TAKING CONTROL

New Hope for Substance Abusers and Their Families

FRANK MINIRTH, PAUL MEIER,
SIEGFRIED FINK, WALTER BYRD,
&
DON HAWKINS

Copyright 1988 by
Baker Book House Company

ISBN: 0-8010-6234-9

Third printing, May 1990

Printed in the United States of America

We gratefully acknowledge
the significant contribution of
Marty Williams Anderson,
whose writing and editing expertise made it possible
for five authors' material on this important subject to
be integrated into one comprehensive whole.

Contents

Introduction

Don Hawkins

Bob was one of the most impressive young men I had ever known. Both his father, a former church worker, and he were members of my congregation. Hardworking and industrious, Bob started a business, guided it to success, and moved to a beautiful home in the suburbs with his charming wife and three lovely children.

As the youngest member of his family, Bob had learned early to find ways of killing pain instead of facing problems head-on. He tended to do this in cycles, and his problem was hidden within his family. As his pastor, I became acquainted with the situation when his father called in the middle of the night, crying, "You've got to help Bob. He's an alcoholic, and his life is falling apart. His wife has finally kicked him out."

Bob is a good example of a Christian who outwardly was a teetotaler but in actuality was an alcoholic. He had been raised in a church background where drinking was considered a deadly sin and drunkenness even worse.

When Bob came to see me, he admitted to having started his drinking early in his teens because of boredom. Eventually, after succumbing to the pressures of a group of people with whom he had become involved, he increased his drinking and started smoking marijuana. Later he started drinking during and after work. Whenever he and his fellow workers

9

finished work, they went out to drink. Ultimately, the point came where they began taking a few six packs to work. At one stage, he even talked his wife into smoking marijuana with him. As a result, however, she became depressed. Finally she became angry and quit.

As a pastor, I had tried to keep up with ways of helping alcoholics, because such problems were not unusual during my twenty years of pastoring. My approach with Bob was to get him involved in two groups at church that could provide support for him during his recovery and to get his wife involved in AL-ANON (for family members of alcoholics) and a women's Bible study.

I began meeting with Bob once a week, and slowly but firmly got him to talk about his underlying feelings that tended to bring on the drinking, feelings that he hadn't been aware were triggering it. I also began an intensive program of discipleship and Scripture memorization with Bob. Bob jumped in to this program running. Over a six-week period, he memorized over fifty verses of Scripture on such subjects as assurance of salvation, God's presence with us, victory, overcoming temptation, overcoming anxiety, and problems of alcohol ("strong drink") given in Proverbs. For two years Bob did very well.

Bob needed even more than I was able to give him however. If I had it to do over again and had I known of a comprehensive Christian hospital unit, I would have suggested that he get help there. After I left the church, I heard that he had begun to have problems again. By that time I had learned the importance of hospitalizing alcoholics in order to fight their many problems on all levels. Bob, however, refused to consider that.

For many the process of overcoming substance abuse is intensely difficult. It's a vicious circle of being "on the wagon— off the wagon." Approaches for cure range from "cast out the demon rum!" to "two-week behavior-modification programs with a couple of two-day follow-ups."

The experience of the Minirth-Meier Clinic has indicated that successful treatment is accomplished by dealing with the many factors involved in substance abuse and taking specific steps that recognize the total person—physically, emotionally, and spiritually. The family too needs to receive counseling, and the aid of the local church needs to be enlisted, in order to see that the problem does not follow the normal pattern and recur in the next generation.

The purpose of this book is not to spend time taking a strong stand against drinking and drugs. The harm they can do permeates the book.

I personally choose not to drink, although I do know dedicated Christians who drink occasionally. I also know sincere Christians who think they are not abusing alcohol but who are—just as there are sincere Christians who take Librium, Valium, and other minor tranquilizers and prescription drugs who abuse them without realizing it.

I also choose not to take medications, except for a very rare aspirin or a medication deemed absolutely necessary by a doctor and even then, I question the doctor personally regarding its necessity. My reasoning behind this choice is threefold.

First, I consider my body to be the temple of the Holy Spirit. First Corinthians 6:19–20 admonishes us, "Do you not know that your body is a temple of the Holy Spirit, who is in you, whom you have received from God? You are not your own; you were bought at a price. Therefore honor God with your body." I have decided that for me, personally, it would be wrong to run the risk of being mastered by anything.

Second, there is a history in my family of alcohol abuse. My grandfather, a very personable and outgoing leader in the community, had a major alcohol problem. This created havoc in my mother's family for years. Two of my uncles ultimately followed their father's path into problem drinking. I have also seen many people in churches I have pastored who were dealt megadoses of grief because of substance abuse.

Finally, it is my personal conviction that the way to deal with problems is to go up and over them, not away from them. To face problems head-on will ultimately remove the problem and lead to victory. To look for ways to kill the emotional pain a problem presents only produces two problems to deal with. By the time the second problem becomes one of substance abuse and addiction, the little willpower runners-from-pain possessed originally has diminished to an infinitesimal amount. They need outside help to build the strength of character and outlook to even consider the up-and-over approach.

Encouragers of addicts are fond of quoting 1 Corinthians 10:13, "No temptation has seized you except what is common to man. And God is faithful; he will not let you be tempted beyond what you can bear. But when you are tempted, he will also provide a way out so that you can stand up under it." This verse will not provide a pat answer, however, for looking for, finding, and implementing God's "way out" of heavily tempting situations. It provides, instead, a motivating promise for developing over time a pattern for facing temptations successfully, one that must be practiced in less tempting situations before it can be used in critical ones.

The successful use of God's way out and way to endure include placing a premium on personal responsibility. That is learned with help and support from others; if not from parents in younger years, then from specially trained helpers in controlled circumstances later on.

Using one's will is like using a muscle. If you haven't used and developed it over a long period of time, it isn't going to be of much use in critical situations. The will is God-given but willpower is something you develop through personal choices, big and small, over the years. For Christians, of course, the potential power of the will is even greater, as they learn how to rely on the Holy Spirit for added strength of will. That reliance, however, is a learned reaction. In hard situations, it doesn't come on spontaneously when reliance on the Holy Spirit hasn't been practiced previously under less-pressured circumstances. A lot of what Christian substance-abuse therapy provides can be classified as spiritual and emotional muscle building.

If you have no problems in these areas but want to help people who do, we trust this book will be a great help. At the same time, let us caution you, as we caution ourselves, not to think that you could never have a problem in this or some other debilitating area. Just prior to God's "way out" promise of 1 Corinthians 10:13 are the words, "If you think you are standing firm, be careful that you don't fall!" (1 Cor. 10:12).

To help a substance abuser or addict isn't easy, but it is the goal of this book to help addicts, their families, and others who care for them to deal directly and successfully with a problem that could rob them of life itself.

1

The Problem
We Refuse to Face

Amy was wheeled into the emergency ward, a glassy stare in her eyes. Looking into her face, it seemed as if the real person was no longer present; she was there—but she wasn't there. This young teenager had experienced a bad reaction to the drug known as PCP or angel dust. Her mother and dad stood by in anguish, praying as they sobbed.

Day after day, one of us worked with her in the hospital's psychiatric unit. Antipsychotic medication was administered but nothing worked. Finally, we transferred Amy to a long-term care facility for the mentally ill. We and her distraught parents realized that apart from a direct miracle of God, there was little likelihood that Amy would ever be the same again. She would be diagnosed psychotic for life.

Waiting Too Long

For some time, Amy's parents had been concerned about the direction their only child's life had taken. Much of the time

15

she was lethargic, but they believed this to be true of many teenagers so tried to dismiss their concerns. At times Amy was her old bubbly self, even more excited about life than they had known her to be before.

Their worries ebbed and flowed, as they convinced one another that the changes in their daughter were nothing but growing pains. Only a few weeks before they brought her into the hospital, completely spaced out to her surroundings, had they begun to realize that they must take some kind of action. They could no longer trust Amy's assurances that she wasn't in any kind of trouble or danger. But their indecisiveness and then their delay in action and in knowing exactly what to do caught up with them. They found her, mumbling incoherently in her bedroom, a vial of powder spilled next to her.

Most of us today know the horrors of using many kinds of drugs. And most parents lecture and instruct their children—with what little information they have—of the extreme physical and psychological dangers of such use. On top of that, such chemical substances are known to be illegal. Certainly it would seem that this would be enough to keep normally good, young people away from their use.

And yet for Amy, the only child of a caring, Christian family, somehow this still wasn't enough.

"It's Only Alcohol!"

Other teenagers do stay away from chemical substances but demonstrate their growing independence and approaching adulthood by drinking alcohol instead. Most teenage parties today, if they don't have drugs, at least have alcohol.

Some parents, knowing the horrors of the drug culture, are even relieved when they hear that an offspring has been involved only in drinking. The results of drinking seem mild compared to the seemingly more permanent scars left from chemical substances.

And Robert was one of those. He was a handsome young man, the youngest of five children. He knew enough to stay away from drugs. His parents were committed Christians, active in the church. In fact, Robert had a brother and a sister who went to Bible college and then entered full-time Christian ministries. As a child, Robert had made a profession of faith in Christ as His Savior, too. During subsequent years, however, he found himself struggling with a number of areas, including an overly dependent personality, a volatile temper, and the influence of friends whose values were less than Christian.

In high school Robert started smoking and soon began drinking an occasional can of beer. This led to regular drinking after school and on weekends, and occasionally getting drunk. Frequently, he would come to school with a "buzz," under the influence. At other times, he would drink during school study-hall periods.

His father, sometimes smelling alcohol on his breath, not only lectured him about it but took away privileges. Tearfully promising not to drink again, Robert was usually able to convince his mother to lift the restrictions so that he could carry on with his scheduled activities.

But Robert did drink again—and again. Without realizing it, Robert had become an alcoholic. Whenever he tried to stop he found he couldn't. Realizing he was an alcoholic, he still continued to deny his addiction to others, even beyond high school. After graduation, he lost two jobs, had a beautiful sports car repossessed, and caused his parents endless grief.

Alcohol, Our Worst Drug Problem

The effects of alcohol may seem the lesser of two evils to many, but while illegal drugs affect primarily teenagers and young adults, the long-term effects of addiction to alcohol affect many more individuals, those from a variety of backgrounds and of various ages. Overall the drug of alcohol has a far greater effect on our society than does the often much-more publicized effects of illegal drugs.

Many people still don't realize that alcohol is a drug, officially declared so in the *Diagnostic and Statistical Manual of Mental Disorders III* in 1980, when it categorized alcohol problems with those of other drugs or chemical substances.

While illicit drugs are a major problem in this country, according to the National Commission on Marijuana and Drug Abuse, "Alcohol dependence is without question the most serious drug problem today."

Nearly 70 percent of Americans today drink to one degree or another, the largest percentage ever. An awesome 10 percent of all Americans are considered heavy drinkers, downing two or more drinks (at least 24 ounces of beer, 10 ounces of wine, or three ounces of 86-proof liquor). Even more startling, 10 percent of all drinkers (about 7 percent of the population) will eventually become problem drinkers or alcoholics (Favazza 1983). That is nearly 20 million people, more than six times the number of alcoholics in the USA in 1950, which was only 3 million.

Alcoholism is now the third leading cause of death in America and a major factor in the tenth leading cause (suicide, which is the second leading cause among college students); it also figures in many homicides. Over half of highway automobile deaths are alcohol-related.

Alcohol also leads to death in alcoholics by destroying the bodily organs. Cirrhosis of the liver, hepatitis, delirium tremens (that occur among some long-term alcoholics when they stop drinking) and other results of alcoholism are the direct cause of many deaths.

Such numbers easily belie the idea that most alcoholics are skid-row bums. In fact, half have at least some college education and hold responsible, white-collar jobs (Favazza 1983). While the majority of alcoholics are men, a growing number, 20 to 30 percent or more, are now women.

The number of women alcoholics has always been harder to

identify, since housewives and widows spend long periods of time alone and can more easily hide their drinking problems. Many women die of unknown causes that were undoubtedly alcohol-related, but no one knew about their drinking. However, the growing numbers of women entering the work force, where the effect of their drinking is more open to scrutiny and diagnosis, is now giving us a growing number of definite statistics about women with drinking problems.

The numbers of addicts among other groups are still on the increase as well. While many reports a few years ago communicated that teenagers were staying away from drugs but drinking more alcohol (a relief to some parents), the underlying facts show that one substance usually leads to another. Most teenagers who become involved with alcohol eventually become involved with illegal drugs or vice versa, although they may become more dependent or addicted to one than to the other. Adult addicts tend to be more "loyal" to a favorite drug (or alcohol) while teenager addicts shop around more in their experimentation.

Every year surveys show that a greater percentage of high schoolers regularly take drugs of one sort or another.

Christians and Alcohol

Many Christians assume that such negative statistics apply only to the secular world, people who are not committed to Christian or other religious groups that stress high morals and strong character. However, nearly two-thirds of Protestants now claim to drink at least socially. This means that 10 percent of Protestant drinkers (6 to 7 percent of all church-going Protestants) eventually will be problem drinkers or alcoholics, because the same factors that lead the average American drinker to becoming a problem drinker, as we'll see, also applies to church-going Protestants.

Even the very conservative Christian evangelicals are not immune. In the last two decades, we have seen an increasingly apparent phenomenon, that of the committed Christian evangelical who drinks. Drinking alcoholic beverages socially has become more and more an accepted part of the lifestyle of many Christians.

The fact that only 30 percent of Americans today report that they never drink, a much lower figure than in previous decades, while the growth in percentage of persons who call themselves "born-again" Christians, adds substance to these observations.

As many churches have attempted to specify more positively what spiritual living is, they have stopped emphasizing negative lists of "don'ts" used by churches during the nineteenth and early twentieth centuries. These lists often included "Don't drink." Many older Christians considered a person who drank at all to be a drunkard or, at best, a backslidden Christian.

Evangelicals, who used to be known primarily as a group of teetotalers, no longer hold that distinction. Many evangelicals, particularly upwardly mobile ones, now drink to stay socially relevant in their work and community situations. Acceptance of evangelicals into mainstream America has had the effect of evangelicals' accepting many of mainstream America's social mores. Perhaps too the explosion in the use of other drugs made alcohol seem like a minor risk to health for most people, as society's attention focused on non-liquid and illegal drugs. While a former generation of evangelicals would frequently hear sermons denouncing alcohol (many of which, of course, did not help churchgoers understand alcohol's true threat), today's pulpits rarely mention the subject. It seems that warnings of the dangers of illegal drugs have all but buried this older threat. To Christian and non-Christian alike, drinking alcoholic beverages seems harmless indeed compared with the bizarre stories we hear about the effects of illegal drug taking.

For this and other reasons, today it is not unusual to be offered an alcoholic drink when with a group of conservative Christians, even at a Bible study or other home Christian meeting. The hosts seemingly never consider their offer of such hospitality to be looked at askance or considered anything but a part of healthy Christian fellowship. At least one pastor has been so amazed at the change in outlook on social drinking among evangelicals that he has written *What Will You Have to Drink? The New Christian Password* (Dunn 1980).

The Christian's Need to Know About Drugs

Through our years of working with lives that have been injured or ruined by substance abuse, we have developed a burden to see that Christians—parents, teenagers, teachers, pastors, and physicians—are

1. made more aware of the problem of drugs, including alcohol, in American society and in the Christian society, and
2. educated regarding drug abuse and its (a) prevention; (b) symptoms; (c) dependency; and (d) cure.

Too often in our medical and psychological practices we have seen the tragic results of alcohol and other drugs in Christian families where loved ones of addicts have, perhaps, had questioning flashes of uneasiness about the possibility of a family member's addiction. Such fleeting thoughts are often followed, however, by self-convincing determination that the problems of substance abuse couldn't happen within *their* families. They understand far too little about the physical, psychological, and spiritual vulnerabilities to alcohol and other drugs that exist in many of our lives, or how to guard against these becoming an entangling, destructive force.

With this mind-set, they take too long to realize that dependency or approaching dependency on alcohol and other drugs *already is* a problem to them and to their families. Then, not knowing what action to take, they wait until (as in

Amy's case) it is too late or (as in Robert's case, as we'll see later) almost too late to put injured lives—the addict's and those of his or her family members—back together again.

Had they known and heeded the information in this book, we are certain that the story of their families, from one generation to the next, would have had a far-different ending.

2

From Use to Abuse

A century ago, Sigmund Freud recorded the words: "I took for the first time 0.05 grains of cocaine. A few minutes later, I experienced a sudden exhilaration and a feeling of ease" (Gomez 1984).

For years, many people used cocaine legally. In fact, Coca-Cola once contained cocaine (Gomez 1984).

Pushing Cocaine
the Freud and Coca-Cola Way

Although cocaine is now illegal, its abuse was the fastest growing of any drug during the first half of the 1980s. College students and up-and-coming so-called yuppies involved in the social fad to experience the intense high of cocaine often passed around the stories about Freud and about Coca-Cola to prove not only cocaine's benefits but its innocence. They also widely publicized the fact that cocaine is not physically addicting.

Rarely, however, did the cocaine-sniffing "in" crowd think

through why cocaine is now illegal and is no longer contained in Coca-Cola, or tell the story of Freud's friend and patient, whose experience with cocaine was entirely different from Freud's own.

What was good for him, Freud believed, also would be good for his patients, so Freud prescribed cocaine usage for a friend. Under Freud's care, the friend became addicted to cocaine, and for the rest of his life hallucinated "white snakes" on his body (Gomez 1984).

While physical dependency upon cocaine is not considered to be a problem, the research of the past few years has found that *psychological* dependency on cocaine *is* a problem. The short, intense high of cocaine, only a few minutes long, is usually followed by a low. To avoid this low, repeated doses of cocaine are often taken.

A newer, more potent form of cocaine is smoked. Called "crack" within the drug culture, it is physically as addictive as heroin. Crack goes straight from the lungs to the heart and creates a strain on the heart that can quickly produce death. The deaths of several well-known physically healthy athletes from crack has given a new outlook on the dangers not only of crack cocaine but of conventional cocaine.

Innocent Mary Jane

Fifteen years before cocaine's reputation of innocence was dispelled, marijuana, or "mary jane," was listed in that category by so-called experts and authorities who pushed for the legalizing of that drug.

Younger people don't realize that we've now gone through several fad cycles of newly discovered or rediscovered drug fads, supposedly harmless ones, which are considered safe only because there haven't been enough people or enough time pass to research their long-term effects properly. Only after numerous lives have been destroyed by these so-called safer drugs have their real dangers become apparent.

Personally, we have seen teenagers admitted into the hospitals we staff experiencing fear, anxiety, apprehension, and even psychoses, all a result of their use of the once-dubbed innocent marijuana.

Marijuana's popularity began among college students in the early 1960s, spreading explosively into an epidemic involving all regions of the country. By the mid-1970s, its use was epidemic among high schoolers, and by the early 1980s it was fairly common even among fifth and sixth graders.

A Dallas, Texas, high school in an upper-class area recently revealed statistics showing that 75 percent of the students drink alcohol, 25 percent smoke marijuana, and 10 percent use cocaine.

Today's marijuana is a greater danger than that used a few years ago, since the weed from which marijuana cigarettes is made has now been hybrid-grown to include up to ten times more tetrahydrocannabinols (THC) than did the original marijuana weed ("The Kinds of Drugs" 1984). This THC is absorbed into the fatty tissue of the brain, never to come out. Marijuana is further discussed in chapter 3.

Of course statistics often mean little to teenagers. They generally think of themselves as indestructible, since the limitations of their overall health have yet to be tested.

Young people abuse drugs for many reasons. Many face the breakup of a family. Others face the breakdown of a support system—friends, teachers, and relatives—because of frequent moves in our mobile society. In our fast and furious world, many rarely have the attention of their parents. All are trying to cope with the physical and emotional changes of adolescence. Drugs may build confidence, relieve anxiety, allow temporary escape from responsibility, calm hostility, and allow emotional regression backward to a time when their lives experienced fewer areas of stress that they needed to make personal decisions about. They present a negative way to gain attention from parents and/or peers. Finally, young people, not wanting to appear immature or cowardly, often lack the moral conviction and spiritual fortitude to just say no.

Since drugs will alter our consciousness, they will stop any of our feelings for a while. People have even taken drugs to stop suicidal feelings, hunger feelings, anger feelings, and so forth. However, once the feeling has been stopped for a while, once the drug wears off, the original feeling comes back stronger than ever.

There is a lie of the devil that a drug may be good for you because it gives you immediate relief. But it is like a man falling from a tall building. He may think, at first, that he is flying, that there is no problem—he is floating through the air—but then there is the sickening crash as he eventually hits the bottom.

"Just One Taste Won't Hurt"

Teenagers aren't the only ones to experiment with drugs and then be caught up with them however. Older adults do, too—some who never thought they would be "caught dead near the stuff!"

Like teenagers, their first try of a drug may be

1. Out of curiosity.
2. Out of rebellion.
3. To be considered one of the group in which they find themselves, or not to embarrass themselves by saying no.
4. Because their defenses against alcohol or other drugs have been penetrated. For instance, some people raised in strict alcoholic-abstinence settings have vague, illogical assumptions that anyone who drinks only one drink will readily appear less than alert, less than healthy, less than controlled, and will act unbecomingly. When faced with other seemingly happy, healthy people consuming a drug, it doesn't seem as dangerous as they had thought. Then when they try it and find it produces (initially) a feeling of elation, they assume that everything

they ever heard about the substance was wrong. They begin to consume it freely and soon find themselves dependent upon it.

5. On the advice of a friend or counselor (including a physician) to help escape some particular stresses they are experiencing. In the case of adults, this would more likely include legal drugs—alcohol, prescription drugs, or over-the-counter drugs. From occasional consumption, usually with other people, over time the person may want an unlimited supply to take compulsively, often when alone.

Drug use begins to change to drug abuse when getting high becomes a goal in itself, rather than as a part of "being sociable." Drug abuse changes to drug dependency when getting high becomes not just a goal but *the* goal of life. Drug dependency's last stage is when the user never feels good except when taking the drug. He or she takes the drug just to feel okay.

Response to Stress
Determines Dependency

From abuse to dependency almost always begins during the experiencing of current stress—the particular stresses of the moment. The way chosen to change, escape, or lift the bad feelings that a stressful situation produces is the consumption of drugs. Dependency begins when their chemicals are *needed* in order to feel good at all.

Symptoms of Chemical Dependency

A teenager who is abusing drugs may exhibit the following behavior:

1. Deterioration in school performance and other school activities.
2. Deterioration in family relationships, including such things as avoidance of family activity and refusal to do chores.
3. Listening to different music. The piper is playing his music today. Some people may disagree, but the kind of music a person likes tells a lot about his inner feelings and life-style.
4. Negative personality changes such as no motivation, depression, or "conning" behavior, unpredictable mood swings from sluggishness in thought processes to over-enthusiastic jabbering, depending on whether the drugs are in or out of their system.
5. Physical changes that might include frequent sore throat, cough, red eyes, occasional droopy eyes, and lack of emotions. The physical assessment should also note hair length, dress style, and signs that the adolescent is getting his messages from the drug culture.

   There may be a change in sleep pattern, beginning to sleep later and later. They want to be more reclusive and spend more time alone at odd hours. Sometimes they will retreat for a whole afternoon, when there are really many more fun things to do with old friends or family.

   The physical changes may come not as early as the social changes because the teenage body is so strong that it can resist physically early on.
6. Legal problems, including missing money at home, shoplifting, vandalism, and traffic problems.
7. Change in peer group, especially if it includes young people the parents feel uncomfortable about or have never met.

Symptoms of Alcoholism

A person may be considered to have gone from alcoholic abuse to alcoholism when there is:

1. *Physical dependency on alcohol, which is manifested by withdrawal symptoms when intake is interrupted.* These are characterized by a state of anxiety and physical trembling between eight to twelve hours after withdrawal from alcohol. Irritability, gastrointestinal upset, and vague discomfort are common. An alcoholic who tries to cease drinking on his own, when encountering these symptoms of withdrawal over a couple of hours, is likely to start drinking again, since alcohol will relieve the withdrawal symptoms.

Anyone who experiences these early alcohol withdrawal symptoms should be hospitalized before continuing the withdrawal, in order to have proper treatment available in case more severe reactions should occur later on in the withdrawal. For some, usually the more advanced cases, these may include grand mal seizures after forty-eight hours, mild hallucinations by the third day, and delirium tremens (d.t.'s) on the fourth or fifth day, which is considered a medical emergency as major as a heart attack.

2. *Diminished ability to function appropriately socially or occupationally due to alcohol* (violent acts, absence from work, legal difficulties, driving while intoxicated, loss of job, and conflicts with family and friends).

3. *Tolerance to the desired effects of alcohol.* More and more alcohol must be consumed in order to produce the desired high, state of relaxation, and so forth.

4. *Continued drinking despite serious medical complications.*

5. *Alcohol-associated illnesses:* cirrhosis of the liver, cerebellar brain degeneration, gastritis, hepatitis, blood coagulation disorders, neuropathy, chronic brain syndrome affecting thought functions, and for infants of alcoholic women, fetal alcohol syndrome (low birth weight, mental retardation, birth defects).

6. *Patterns of psychological alcohol use—need for daily use of alcohol to function;* inability to decrease or stop drinking despite repeated efforts; drinking early in the morning, and blackouts.

7. *Unpleasant physical tell-tale signs:* alcohol odor on the breath, flushed face, tremor, injuries of vague origin.

8. *At least one month's duration of disturbance of three or more of the above* (ed., Krupp and Chatton 1981; "The Kinds of Drugs" 1984; Tomb 1981; Mirin 1977; Meyer 1980).

Of course, most people who try or occasionally participate in taking alcohol or some other type of drug socially never become abusers. So how can you know if someone is likely to become an abuser? While you can't know if you or someone close to you will ever become an actual abuser or addict, there are some factors of vulnerability that if combined with enough other factors, are likely to "drive a person to drink, or to other drugs" rather than to drive him or her toward healthier solutions to personal problems.

David, the Pampered Teenager

Take David, for instance. David lived with his mother and stepfather. His mother, a Christian, had never been around alcohol until she married David's stepdad, who was a social drinker. To comply with social pressures, David's mom became a social drinker, too. Social drinking led to increased drinking by both parents, particularly at home on weekends.

Both parents tended to protect David whenever he had trouble in school or with the law. They were always quick to bail him out of trouble, and were always hesitant to rebuke or punish him. They furnished him with everything that he wanted—money, clothes, and a car.

Modeling the pattern of his parents, David had begun drinking in his early teens. To escape the normal ups-and-downs of adolescent emotions, he began to run to the liquor cabinet. By his midteen years, he and his family realized that he was indeed an alcoholic.

The overprotective pattern on the part of both parents, in which David had no opportunity to learn self-discipline or self-responsibility, coupled with the observed pattern of parental drinking in the home, had resulted in David's alcoholism.

This was his state when he first came to us for treatment.

The Search for Outside Help

Drug abuse and dependency, we believe, usually (but not always) has a lot to do with how independent a person truly is before they first become involved with a drug. Are they self-sufficient, accepting blame for their own mistakes and used to finding answers for their problems themselves? Or do they blame their problems, not on themselves, but on other people? Do they usually look to someone else to get them out of their problems?

While the factor of the passive-dependent personality in addictions has been a controversial one in medical and psychological circles, our experience in treating thousands of drug-dependent individuals has proved to us that the large majority do come out of a family setting that has molded them into this passive-dependent outlook on themselves and on life. We will discuss this personality type and others that may be addiction-prone in a later chapter and the Appendix.

A Way to Escape

If individuals have never been taught self-sufficiency *and* self-assurance, they are more likely, when they can't find a human personal problem-solver, a mother-substitute, to try to "find their answers in a bottle" or other drug container. Once they have been introduced to the feelings of escapism that a drug can give, those people who have not learned how to be successfully dependent on themselves will more than likely look for "a way to escape" than a way to tackle and conquer a problem head-on. They will choose a way out rather than a way up and over.

Old and New Christian Outlooks

Well-instructed Christians of "the old school" will immediately sense that "a way up and over" falls right in line with traditional Christian thinking, with living a "victorious Christian life." Those who do choose a way out (substance abuse) instead of the way "up and over" are likely to be judged dogmatically as sinners in need of repentance. Old-school Christians believe that once "truly repentant," addicts will then just kick their habit and become productive Christians and citizens.

Other Christians, who consider themselves up-to-date with the latest scientific findings, will disagree vehemently with this last statement, declaring that alcoholism and even other drug dependencies are really a disease. The addict needs to be helped medically, not preached to.

Disputes between these two extremes has left many a church helping addicts that come their way in no way at all, either because of approaching the problem from one of these extremes only or by indecisively trying to straddle the fence in their approach to the problem.

Helping individuals and churches find the complete, comprehensive way—physically, psychologically, and spiritually—to cure the addict (and those close to the addict, who have been greatly damaged by the addict's behavior), as well as to prevent others from becoming addicts, is our reason for writing this book.

3

Types of Drugs

The kinds of addictive substances that are destroying our lives include both the types that scare most people and the types that we consider to be part of our everyday way of life.

While many readers will read this book to look for help for themselves or for loved ones whom they suspect take the supposedly "harder" drugs, they may not realize they are leading themselves and their loved ones toward a traumatic battle over their own health on down the road. Why? Because of their personal addiction to the everyday substances that are harmful and dependency-producing: *caffeine, tobacco,* and even the *binging of food.*

Drugs are ruining the health of our present generation of young people. In many cases, their minds and bodies will never be the same. For the rest of their lives, some will just seem dull mentally, others will have no motivation, others will be depressed or psychotic, and some will die from resulting medical diseases.

Others of us, usually adults, will ruin our health through the more innocent drugs.

Sally, the Dependent, Love-starved
Pastor's Wife

Take Sally, for instance. Sally was a pastor's wife who was
quite dependent on her mother while she was growing up. Her
father was a pastor himself, very busy serving God and his
church, who had little time for his children. As a result, Sally
craved her father's affection. This two-fold parental dilemma
is common among addictive-prone personalities.

Sally became strongly attracted to Steve, a theology student, because he reminded her of her father in many ways. He
was a good person and a good pastor.

Because he did have tendencies like Sally's dad, once they
were married, Steve too ended up spending a lot of time away
from his home and family, throwing himself into church work
and the supposed needs of his parishioners to the neglect of
the needs of his family.

As their marriage and family grew, Sally became more
and more depressed. At age forty, Sally had repressed anger
toward everyone in her life. She was angry toward Steve for
not meeting her needs for attention and affection, which
really started with resentment toward her father for not meeting these needs.

At the same time, Sally was dependent on others for her
self-worth, as she had been upon her mother in childhood. She
also was passive, so didn't share her true feelings, holding
them in for fear of being rejected by others. As a result, she let
church members control her. Then she turned around and
asked for more control by volunteering for church responsibilities that no one else wanted, which she rationalized was her
responsibility as a good pastor's wife. As a result, she resented
church members who allowed her to take on disliked and de-
meaning responsibilities. But she never told anyone how she
felt. She acted as if she desired to be the suffering saint.

Sally's repressed anger (which produced depression) eventually turned to rage—at the church, at her husband, and at

her father. She was afraid of being aware of her rage, however, so she became increasingly anxious as well as depressed.

It's Only Medication

To overcome her anxiety and depression, Sally's family doctor prescribed Valium. Taking Valium made her feel more relaxed, but did not help her depression. (In fact, this drug makes many individuals' depression worse by lowering the serotonin level in their brains.) Taking more and more Valium in order to create the same amount of relaxation she experienced when she first started taking it (a quality of all addictive drugs), Sally went back to her doctor to get a larger amount of Valium pills. Her doctor, knowing Valium's addictive qualities, told her she could take only a certain amount per day.

As a result, Sally went to another doctor, and then another and another, in order to get more prescriptions for Valium. She got each filled at a different pharmacy and became a strong Valium abuser.

Finally, Steve began to realize that Sally was continually groggy and concluded that something was wrong. He persuaded her to get help and so she was admitted to one of the hospitals that our clinic helps to staff.

The Need to Know

If we personally and our churches are to become more knowledgeable about drugs, their harm, and what to do about them, we need to educate ourselves and others about the types of drugs available and their effects, from the ones we all have used for years to the ones that are too new to diagnose their dangers yet.

1. *Alcohol—the most commonly abused drug in America.* It has been estimated that almost half of all male high-school

seniors have an alcohol problem ("The Kinds of Drugs" 1984).
Over five thousand teenagers are killed yearly in auto acci-
dents due to drunken driving ("The Kinds of Drugs" 1984).

Initially, alcoholic consumption results in liveliness and a
sense of well-being. However, with continued consumption,
irritability, emotional instability, and incoordination result.
Coma and even death can occur. Chronic alcoholism can result
in ulcers, anemia, hypertension, cirrhosis, pancreatitis, neuropathy, and brain degeneration. If one has drunk alcohol to
the point he has developed a tolerance (needs greater amounts
to reach the desired "high") then he may go into d.t.'s (delirium tremens) upon ceasing his drinking, with a 15 percent
chance of death from d.t.'s.

"Downers"

Central-nervous-system depressants or "downers" are barbiturates, benzodiazepines, methaqualone, glutethamide,
and methaprylon. They produce physical dependence (Senay
1985, Part 1).

Users typically abuse these drugs for their sedative and intoxicating effects, but some people use them to increase the
effects of another drug such as heroin. Or users may resort to
downers to counteract the negative effect of stimulant drugs
like cocaine (Senay 1985, Part 3).

2. *Barbiturates*—such as seconal and nembutal—are a
type of sedative. They relieve anxiety. Although they are a
prescription drug, many of these "downers" are also sold on
the streets as "yellow jackets," "reds," and "barbs." The liver
metabolizes these drugs and with the help of hepatic enzymes
develops a tolerance for them; as tolerance develops, the
abuser must increase the barbiturate dose needed to produce
the desired effect. Reactions to severe barbiturate intoxication include disorientation, sleeplessness, flaccid muscles,
decreased reflexes, hypotension (abnormally low blood pressure), shock, pulmonary edema (fluid on the lungs), pneu-

monia, and coma. The highest mortality rate is among abusers who overdose on short-acting barbiturates (Giannini,
Price, & Giannini 1986).

Barbiturates produce an addiction occurring after three
to four weeks of daily use of doses, after which an abrupt
discontinuation of them can result in grand mal seizures.
Other withdrawal symptoms include apprehension; weakness; tremor; abnormally low blood pressure; nausea;
twitches; inability to think, respond, and behave realistically
(psychosis); and delirium. Barbiturates are the most common
cause of suicidal death in women (Wharton 1983).

3. *Nonbarbiturate sedatives:* Quaalude, Miltown, Equanil,
Doriden, Placidyl, and others—are also addictive. Doriden
especially has high abuse potential. Quaalude can be very
dangerous, causing a suppressed vomit reflex, fixed pupils,
and even a flat brain wave. Coma has occurred with overdoses
of 2.4 g. Treatment of overdose is difficult because Quaalude
or Methaqualone ("lude" as it's called on the streets) is stored
in body fat (Giannini, Price, & Giannini 1986).

Meprobamate (Equanil or Miltown), called "bams" and
"Uncle Milties" on the streets, is among the most abused
drugs possessing sedative-hypnotic properties. The lethal
meprobamate dose varies from 12 to 40 grams; the usual
prescribed dosage of meprobamate is 800 mg. per day in two
to four doses. Slightly higher doses than these taken over
duration can lead to dependence and withdrawal symptoms
(Giannini, Price, & Giannini 1986).

Ethchlorvynol (Placidyl) is a frequently abused drug with
only a small margin of safety. Deaths have occurred after
users took three to six times the average daily dosage of
this drug. Placidyl's street names are "Mr. Green Jeans,"
"pickles," and "jellybeans" (Giannini, Price, & Giannini
1986).

Ethchlorvynol's effect is fast but brief (about three hours).
Blood levels peak sixty to ninety minutes after the drug is ingested. Clinical studies of ethchlorvynol overdose reveal
symptoms such as cardiac arrest, depression, hypotension,

hypothermia (subnormal body temperature), pulmonary edema, and respiratory arrest (Giannini, Price, & Giannini 1986).

4. *Benzodiazepine,* like Valium, is also one of the most commonly abused sedative drugs. For thirteen years it was the number-one prescribed drug (recently surpassed by Cimetidine for ulcers). Benzodiazepines are referred to on the street as "Roches," "tranks" and "pumpkin seeds." They, too, are addicting and thus require an ever-increasing dose to produce relief of anxiety. And they also result in withdrawal symptoms on cessation. Benzodiazepine taken along with alcohol, propoxyphene (Darvon) or other central-nervous-system depressants can result in death. Reactions to an acute benzodiazepine overdose include nystagmus (rapid involuntary movement of the eyeballs), ataxia (inability to coordinate voluntary muscle movements), confusion, slurred speech, hypotension and depressed respiration. Withdrawal should always be carried out gradually because abrupt discontinuance of a benzodiazepine can result in severe withdrawal symptoms such as convulsions or psychosis (Giannini, Price, & Giannini 1986).

5. *Sleeping pills* fall in the category of sedatives. They include Dalmane, Restoril, Halcion, and Seconal.

6. *Bromides* were used for years as sedatives. They were used in such over-the-counter medications as Miles Nervine. We remember one woman admitted to a psychiatric unit in a psychotic state. She had felt some anxiety and had turned to a popular, easily obtained bromide for relief. She developed, as some people do on too much bromide, a psychosis (an inability to distinguish reality). Once the substance was cleaned out of her body, however, her thought processes returned to normal.

Tranquilizers, Antidepressants, and OTC Drugs

Tranquilizers, antidepressants, and over-the-counter (OTC) drugs are not typically used as primary drugs of abuse, but they are used to enhance the intoxicating effects of primary drugs of abuse, such as "boosting the high" of heroin (Senay 1985, Part 1).

7. *Over-the-counter sleeping pills* are used by thousands of young and old people alike. They usually contain an antihistamine, which produces a sedative effect. However, they too are not without side-effects. One man came to our clinic in a psychotic state who had been taking many of these pills.

Other *minor tranquilizers* include Xanax, Librium, Serax, Tranxene, and Centrax.

Narcotics

8. *Opiate Drugs*—narcotics—like heroin, morphine, codeine, meperidine, methadone, paregoric, elixir, terpinhydrate, Dilaudid, Hycodan, Percodan, Demerol, Darvon, and Talwin are all addictive. The opium-addiction rate was high in America in the early 1900s before the passage of the Harrison Act, which restricted its use (Dougherty and Rush 1982).

Opium, derived from the sap of the wild poppy, is refined to form morphine and heroin. Synthetic opiates—meperidine, propoxyphene, and pentazocine—are also widely abused. Heroin's street names include "horse," "skag," "smack," and "boy" (Giannini, Price, & Giannini 1986).

In the central nervous system opiates block mu and delta endorphin receptors, which have been discovered to be involved in a wide range of psychiatric disorders, including depression, mania, and schizophrenia. Endorphins are also responsible for many of the signs and symptoms seen in withdrawal and opiate intoxication, such as pulmonary edema, respiratory depression, and coma (Giannini, Price, & Giannini 1986).

With an overdose of *heroin,* one has depressed respiration, depressed consciousness, pinpoint pupils, extremely low blood pressure, and fluid in the lungs. Heroin withdrawal symptoms, on the other hand, include increased respiration, sweating, tremor, irritability, nausea, dilated pupils, and cramps.

Heroin is an extremely deadly drug among our youth. It usually follows a period of "polydrug use" and often dominates the individual's lifestyle. The craving for the substance often leads to theft to obtain funds to further the habit. Only one of every three heroin addicts lives past the age of thirty-five.

Today, when most of us think of heroin we think of the back streets of some large city, of hard-drug addicts among our youth, and of the Mafia. And yet many narcotics are abused through prescription drugs (Dougherty and Rush 1982). Many derivatives of opium originally thought not to be addicting have proven otherwise. They include morphine, Demerol, Darvon, and Talwin.

Demerol is the leading narcotic of addiction among nurses and doctors. *Hycodan* comes in table syrup and has abuse potential. *Darvon* for pain (and associated with withdrawal seizures) is abused widely. *Talwin* for pain is in demand because of the "big rush" it produces. *Methadone,* used to treat heroin addicts, is itself addicting (Mirin 1977).

Stimulants

Stimulants include cocaine and amphetamines, and they have an original phase of stimulation, although all drugs eventually depress the nervous system (Senay 1985, Part 3).

9. *Cocaine* is the fastest growing abused drug today ("The Kinds of Drugs" 1984). Street names for it are "coke," "white girl," and "toot." Cocaine attracts considerable attention from the public because it is a popular drug among the wealthy in American society and has drained the lives of prominent sports figures, film stars, and wealthy businessmen (Giannini, Price, & Giannini 1986).

Cocaine comes from the leaves of the coca plant and is usually taken by snorting it through the nostrils. Users who "snort" low doses of cocaine hydrochloride (15–25 mg.) usually report feeling more confident, more energetic, more powerful and/or more relaxed, but as the dose increases each time they use it, these feelings may give way to paranoia, hypervigilance, suspiciousness, and sometimes to psychotic behavior, occasionally marked by violence (Senay 1985, Part 3).

Sometimes cocaine is smoked in a form called *freebase,* which greatly increases the drug's concentration. Freebasing involves freeing cocaine from cocaine hydrochloride (its usual form) and then smoking the more concentrated freebase. "Basing" (smoking freebase) as opposed to "snorting" cocaine results in a much higher dose affecting the brain. Someone snorting hydrochloride might use a dose of 400–500 mg. in an evening but a user "basing" might smoke 14,000–28,000 mg. of cocaine. The drug is hallucinogenic and a psychotogen at these high doses. Freebase users report memory and judgment impairment, paranoid states, and intense depression during withdrawal (Senay 1985) as well as anxiety, anorexia, fatigue, sad mood, irritability, insomnia, nausea, diarrhea, diaphoresis (artificially induced perspiration), and myalgia (muscular pain) (*Currents in Affective Illness* April 1987).

Cocaine produces an intense high for a few minutes. However, this high is usually followed by a low. Repeated doses are often taken to avoid the low. Some cocaine users take alcohol, heroin, marijuana, or any of the central-nervous-system depressants to counteract the extreme discomfort resulting from high doses of cocaine (Senay 1985). Heavy cocaine intake is similar to acute amphetamine intoxication in that both drugs at first stimulate the heart rate and blood pressure. But the reactions following this are circulatory failure, convulsions, respiratory failure, and coma, as well as psychotic states, hallucinations, and paranoia (Giannini, Price, & Giannini 1986).

Complications of cocaine include irritability, lassitude, hallucinations, anxiety attack, delusions, convulsions, and even death. Physical dependency is not a major problem, except in the case of crack, but psychological dependency is.

Users of cocaine (especially basers) often seek treatment much earlier than users of other kinds of drugs. Cost is a common reason for this: Cocaine costs about one hundred dollars per gram, and smoking one-half an ounce of freebase per day costs fifteen hundred dollars. Other reasons include friction with family and in social relationships, and impaired judgment (Senay 1985, Part 2).

10. *Amphetamines,* central-nervous-system stimulants, usually referred to as "uppers," are the drugs health-care professionals abuse (Giannini, Price, & Giannini 1986). The drugs have been widely used medically for weight reduction and mood elevators but have also been frequently used by truck drivers and students to combat drowsiness and fatigue. This background of use, combined with the euphoria they produce, have made them very popular drugs of abuse among young people. They can be taken orally or intravenously. Other street names for these include "bennies," "uppers," "diet pills," "double crosses," "black beauties," "Christmas trees," and "speedball" (amphetamine or cocaine with an opioid). When methylated, amphetamine becomes methamphetamine, sold under the names "speed," "crystal," "meth" and "white crosses." Phenylpropanolamine hydrochloride, contained in many sinus tablets and diet pills, is similar to amphetamines and is often substituted for them. It comes from the leaves of a green plant called khat (Giannini, Price, & Giannini 1986).

Tolerance for amphetamines develops quickly and a larger and larger dosage is required in order to experience the "rush" like feeling. Amphetamines work on the alpha and beta receptors and thus may induce hazardous cardiovascular reactions. With acute intoxication one may see sweating, rapid heart beat, elevated blood pressure, hyperactivity, confusion, and even psychosis, as well as suppressed appetite, accelerated thinking, increased sex drive, decreased desire to sleep, and a feeling of excitement. The amphetamine abuser often loses respect for authority and ability to perceive errors and becomes belligerent (Giannini, Price, & Giannini 1986).

In the early stages of amphetamine psychosis, there is euphoria and talkativeness. Next there may be teeth grinding, picking movements, time distortions, suspiciousness, and increased aggressiveness. Later there are persecutory delusions, hallucinations, hyperactivity, stereotyped compulsivity, and unstable mood.

Physical symptoms of amphetamine intoxication include rapid heart beat, increased blood pressure, pupillary dilation, chills, nausea, and insomnia. Other stimulants, other than amphetamines, which produce similar results are Dexedrine, preludin, and cocaine.

Not only can these drugs produce a psychosis but, in many cases, they will cause a rebound depression in a couple of weeks. Suicide is a danger during this time. Profound fatigue, irritability, anxiety, nightmares, and insomnia are often symptoms of this depression.

11. *Marijuana.* Now known to be an extreme health hazard, marijuana is still the most widely used illegal drug in the USA. An estimated quarter of the population has tried it and 20 million people in the USA smoke it daily, including preteens and many persons working in industry (Nicholi, "Marijuana").

Among college students, marijuana is second only to alcohol as the drug of abuse, and more than 25 million Americans over the age of 12 have tried it. More than 50 street names for the drug, including "Acapulco gold," "grass," "pot," "weed," "hashish," "bhang," "ganja," "charas," "dogga," and "mary jane" suggest its widespread use in American society. Marijuana comes from the leafy green plant, *Cannabis sativa,* grown wild in most parts of the United States and South America. The plant contains the active ingredient, delta-9-tetrahydro-cannabinol (THC) (Giannini, Price, & Giannini 1986). Cannabis comes in two forms: ordinary marijuana (pot) and hashish. The difference between them is in dose. Pot has 2 to 10 mg. of THC per unit (a joint) and hashish has two to three times that amount (Senay 1985, Part 1).

Cannabis or marijuana is usually smoked, but it is also eaten. Small doses of the drug induce mild euphoria, psychosedation and motor retardation, and larger doses may cause feelings of depersonalization, hallucinations, and paranoia (Giannini, Price, & Giannini 1986). Recent findings challenge the past notion that marijuana does not produce physical or psychological dependence. Research conducted by Reese Jones at Stanford University indicates that marijuana can produce dependence. Patients smoking from five to thirty joints a day said they were compelled to smoke marijuana even though they realized the negative consequences and that they had lost control over when and how much they used (Senay 1985, Part 3).

As mentioned before, today's marijuana is much more dangerous than the marijuana of a decade or more ago, containing ten times the amount of tetrahydrocannabinol (THC) than it did a few years ago ("The Kinds of Drugs" 1984). This THC is absorbed into the fatty tissue of the brain never to come out. It bears repeating that research has shown that individuals who have smoked at least two cigarettes of marijuana per day for two years have abnormal brain wave readings and also have corresponding behavioral changes (such as chronic lethargy and loss of inhibition). Regular users of marijuana (once or twice per week) show evidence of memory impairment, sleep disturbance, and swings of mood. In general, they function at a lower level.

Marijuana contains over four hundred known chemicals with many effects ("The Kinds of Drugs" 1984). Not only are there adverse effects on the brain but also on the heart and lungs. It is high in cancer-causing agents. It is absorbed into the fatty tissue of the gonads and decreases testosterone production (men become more feminine). Marijuana alters cellular defenses against disease with the reduction of the white-blood-cell count. Reaction time is reduced significantly. There is a danger of THC passing from an expectant mother to her unborn child.

12. *Hallucinogens.* These drugs include LSD; STP; mescaline (peyote) from cactus; psilocybin from mushrooms; DMT; morning glory seeds; nutmeg; stramonium; and MDMA or "ecstasy." All of the hallucinogens affect the pons and de-

crease neuronal firing and serotonin turnover (Giannini, Price, & Giannini 1986). Some hallucinogens such as STP may have effects which the user cannot turn off for a period of twenty-four to thirty-six hours including serious impairment in judgment (Senay 1985, Part 3).

Many of these hallucinogens (PCP, LSD, mescaline, psilocybin, marijuana) produce bad trips ("The Kinds of Drugs" 1984; ed., Krupp and Chatton 1981). Bad trips occur when the actual drug effects deviate from the desired ones. Dangerous trips often occur with the following drugs.

PCP (phencyclidine, also known as "angel dust," "porker," "zoom," "Sherman," "peace pill," "superpot," "hog") was developed as an anesthetic agent in veterinary practice. It was abandoned for human use when the bizarre effects it produces in people were discovered. PCP distorts reality in ways that resemble serious mental disorders. It produces an initial euphoria accompanied by a feeling of numbness, which is only the lull before the storm. Soon afterwards it may cause disorientation, distortions, combativeness, confusion, violence, bizarre behavior, psychosis, increase in blood pressure, seizures, and even death (ed., Krupp and Chatton 1981). This drug is simple to produce and is sometimes sold as marijuana or LSD. It is usually smoked in marijuana cigarettes but can be inhaled, injected or swallowed, rubbed on the tongue, mixed with parsley or oregano or with such drugs as marijuana, or taken as an enema (Giannini, Price, & Giannini 1986).

PCP affects the brain's neurotransmitter receptor system. If the user has taken 5 mg., such symptoms as anxiety, ataxia, excitement, flushing, conceptual disorganization and hallucinations may appear, but if the user has taken 5 to 10 mg., signs and symptoms include fever, amnesia, hyporeflexia, stupor, hypersalivation and coma. More than 10 mg. of PCP can result in delusions, hypertension, convulsions, coma, and death (Giannini, Price, & Giannini 1986).

We have seen several teenagers with a permanent psychosis because of this drug. If a teenager is having a "bad trip" on

PCP, a medical doctor should be called immediately. The patient is usually treated in a quiet, calm setting, and medication called Haldol is often used.

LSD (lysergic acid/diethylamide) has many street names:
It's called "windowpane" in gelatin form; "blotter" when it's
soaked into paper or Mickey Mouse decals called "Mickies";
"microdot" in tablet form; and "Mr. Natural" or "blue devil"
in capsule form (Giannini, Price, & Giannini 1986). LSD
often produces mental symptoms of hyperactivity and pre-
occupation with one's own thoughts and perceptions (ed.,
Krupp and Chatton 1981). There may be an initial feeling of
tension, which may be followed by an emotional release such
as laughing. Later, perceptual distortions, hallucinations,
changes in time sense, mood instability, a feeling of detach-
ment, and a sense of destiny may occur. A dose of 20 to 40 mcg.
of LSD can induce cross-sensory perception, a condition in
which the user hears or tastes colors and smells sounds. This
type of hallucination is not found in functional psychosis.
Other LSD abuse signs and symptoms include blurred vision,
distorted perception of space, time and self-image, mental dis-
sociation, tremors, hyperreflexia, and mood swings. LSD is an
extremely potent drug. A dose of 0.5 mcg. can produce a high
that lasts up to twelve hours in a man weighing 155 pounds
(Giannini, Price, & Giannini 1986).

LSD's effects on behavior are not only long-lasting but also
violent. Erratic behavior often results in injury or death.
Long-term psychosis may result. Panic reactions are a common occurrence. Flashbacks (mental imagery from a previous
bad trip) may occur.

Mescaline is derived from the peyote cactus, a small plant
with soft spikes and small pink or red flowers. Street names
for the drug are "button," "peyote," "mesc," and "moon." Mescaline, since it is rapidly absorbed, causes hallucinations and
temporary psychosis. Users often hallucinate that they are
being followed by marching geometric forms (Giannini, Price,
& Giannini 1986).

Psilocybin, taken from the mushroom, *Psilocybe mexicana,* which grows in Mexico and the USA causes chromatopsia, a condition in which the user perceives black and white to be in color. One or two of the mushrooms ingested in a dried form can produce hallucinogenic effects lasting six hours (Giannini, Price, & Giannini 1986).

DMT (dimethyltryptamine), or "the businessman's lunch," produces hallucinogenic effects that last thirty minutes. DMT's effect is instantaneous after the user inhales or injects the synthetic form (Giannini, Price, & Giannini 1986).

Morning glory seeds are also used as a hallucinogen. Sometimes the seeds are sprayed with paraquat, a toxic herbicide, to discourage their use as a drug. Street names for the seeds are "heavenly gates," "pearly gates," "flying saucers," and "licorice drops" (Giannini, Price, & Giannini 1986).

Drug users who do not know how to manufacture LSD often substitute nutmeg as a hallucinogen. These people are mostly children and adolescents who cannot obtain street LSD. Nutmeg is perhaps the most potent hallucinogen available. A deterrent in the use of nutmeg is that it induces vomiting. In an attempt to avoid this, users sometimes mix nutmeg with cola, a mixture that is referred to as "brown slime" (Giannini, Price, & Giannini 1986).

MDMA or "ecstasy" (3, 4 methylenedioxymethamphetamine), a drug related to both hallucinogens and amphetamines, has recently become popular. It is also referred to as "the businessman's lunch" because it acts rapidly but lasts briefly (Giannini, Price, & Giannini 1986).

13. *Tobacco-use disorder,* surprising to many people, is now included in the classification of mental disorders in *DSM III,* the official psychiatric manual of mental disorders (The American Psychiatric Association 1980).

The chronic use of tobacco predisposes the user to a number of medical diseases (heart disease, lung cancer, bronchitis and emphysema). More than half a million hospital admissions a year are attributed to obstructive lung disease caused by smoking ("Smoking" 1984). It has been estimated that 15 percent of the annual mortality rate in the United States is due to

disease caused by or aggravated by the consumption of tobacco (Rowe 1980). And yet, 37 percent of men and 28 percent
of women in this country smoke ("Smoking" 1984).

14. *Caffeine,* a widely abused drug that is often over-
looked, is like amphetamines in that it affects the central nervous system. Along with alcohol and nicotine, caffeine is
among the most popular mind-affecting drugs. Some ten bil-
lion pounds of coffee are consumed yearly (ed., Krupp and
Chatton 1981). For many, more than 500 to 600 mgm. (four to
five cups of coffee) of caffeine per day can produce anxiety
symptoms (such as tremor or insomnia).

Caffeine can be lethal in some cases. Children have died
after eating less than 1 g. of the drug. A user can get a caffeine
"buzz" from the following: ten No-Doz pills (100 mg. of caffeine per tablet); eight cups of coffee (125 mg. per cup); 12 cups
of tea (80 mg. per cup); or three to five bottles of carbonated
cola (125 mg. per cup) (Giannini, Price, & Giannini 1986).
Withdrawal from caffeine (more than 500 mgm. per day) produces the same symptoms as those of a caffeine overdose:
headaches, irritability, restlessness, tremors, hyperreflexia,
anxiety, abdominal cramps, palpitations, and nausea. A cup
of coffee has 80–140 mgm., tea has 30–80 mgm., and Coca-
Cola has 50 mgm.

15. *Inhalants* include glues, solvents, gasoline, kerosene,
plastic cements, paints, lacquers, enamels, paint thinner,
aerosols, furniture polishes, fingernail polish removers, ni-
trous oxide, and cleaning fluids. The problem of this abuse is
enormous in the United States. It is especially a problem in
adolescence, particularly among lower socioeconomic groups.
It has been estimated that one in every ten persons under age
17 abuse inhalants. Another estimate is that 17 million
Americans are involved in the abuse of inhalants.

While these solvents can produce a mild euphoria, they also
can produce confusion, impulsivity, toxic psychosis, liver disease, kidney disease, bone-marrow suppression, fatigue, anxiety, mood changes, memory difficulties, seizures, coma, and
even death.

The Price of Feeling Good Instantly

We pay a big price in order to get an instant good feeling today. Feeling good *right now* takes precedence over building a healthy body and a healthy mind, over time. Many of us, of course, assume that if we feel good right now, for as long as a drug lasts, we are healthy.

Feeling good chemically, through chemicals that were not meant to be part of the chemical balance of our bodies, is done at a great price. As their temporary high wears off, the imbalance in our spirit, our emotions, and our body, becomes even more evident.

Sally's Better Way of Feeling Good

When Sally, the pastor's wife, was admitted to our hospital ward, we not only treated her physical addiction to Valium and withdrew her from the drug, but we began giving her intensive insight-therapy for ten weeks. During this time she learned to be aware of her grudges toward her father, her husband, and church members. She worked through these grudges; cried about them; asked God's forgiveness for them; forgave all the people who had neglected, used, or emotionally abused her; and forgave herself for being so masochistic.

Sally became more healthily assertive, more aware of her feelings, practiced verbalizing them, and received family therapy, along with her husband. After Sally left the hospital, she and her husband continued in outpatient therapy for nine more months.

Since that time, Sally has become an independent person, although still submitting to her husband's authority in the home. While some people dislike the comparison, we feel that the husband-wife authority in the home can be compared, in many ways, to that of a president and vice president of a company. Previously, Steve and Sally were acting more like president and secretary, or even president and janitor!

Sally even shares her anger now (politely) with her husband, and he shares his (politely) with her. In this way, they
work through their conflicts and have done very well. Their
children, as a result, have improved in their school performance, now that they have a healthy mom and dad.

Steve decreased his church commitments to a point where
he could spend more time with his wife and children, to make
sure that their needs are being met. We pointed out to him the
verse that "he that doesn't take care of the needs of his own
family is worse than an unbeliever" (see 1 Tim. 5:8). We also
showed him that, as a pastor, he doesn't need to do everything
that everyone asks him to do. What he needs to do primarily is
to model for them what a model Christian husband and father
really is. To do this will require him to say no to some of the
desires and demands that the church and individual church
members will want to put on him.

Through a wholistic treatment of the entire person—body,
mind, and spirit—Sally not only was cured of her addiction
to Valium but of her passive-dependent personality tendencies, which had produced her unhappiness and vulnerability to taking addictive substances in order to feel good about
herself.

4

From Sin to Genes

Jerry was special, at least his family thought so. The first of his family to attend college, his older brothers and sisters all helped out on his college expenses to keep him going. Bright and intelligent, Jerry had experienced no trouble with grades in high school. It also helped that he was usually the teacher's pet.

When he got to college, however, Jerry found that his normal last-minute cramming for exams wasn't helping his grades. As he had in high school, he spent most weekends at parties. A couple of semesters later, he realized not only that he had never learned how to study, but also that the few study sessions he started usually ended when he would fall asleep after drinking too much.

In the middle of his sophomore year, Jerry dropped out of college and took a job as a salesman, deeply disappointing his family. His self-image, which had rested on his innate intelligence, took a tumble. He also felt guilty that his family had sacrificed to put him through school, and he had disappointed them. His father arranged a sales position for him with the company he was with.

Although he was a good salesman, using the persuasion techniques he had known from childhood, he would often drink while traveling for his job. Once he was arrested and jailed for driving while intoxicated. Sleeping off his drunkenness in a lock-up cell of the city jail, he awoke on Sunday morning to hear hymn singing. A local church was holding an early Sunday-morning evangelistic service for inmates in another part of the jail. Listening to the service, Jerry came under conviction for his sins and, hearing the invitation to have his sins forgiven and to start a new life in Christ, Jerry prayed. He asked Christ to enter his life as the Savior from his sins.

After being released from jail, Jerry went to visit the pastor who had held the jail service. Ecstatic over Jerry's testimony, the pastor counseled him for a couple of hours and told him of a small church in Jerry's hometown that would be able to help him.

Returning home, Jerry found his way to that church, shared what had happened to him with the pastor, and the following Sunday joined the church. With his unusual testimony and winning personality, Jerry was soon the "life" of church activities, as he had been of collegiate drinking parties a few years before.

Soon several members of his family became Christians and joined the church also, including his sister and brother-in-law.

Not long after that, Jerry found a cute Christian girl in the church and fell head over heels in love. Within a year of their marriage, Jerry and Betty had not one but two babies—twins—a boy and a girl.

Coming home to a chaotic household with a tired wife and two noisy babies soon became hard for Jerry to bear. It was made harder by the fact that for the first time in his life, he was no longer the center of attention in his own home.

Several weeks later, on a business trip, Jerry started drinking. Soon he started drinking regularly in his hotel room in the evenings. As a result, when he was at home, his guilt, coupled with the burden of helping to care for two babies, brought added strife between Jerry and Betty.

Once, while on a business trip, he walked out of the hotel bar late at night with an unsteady gait and walked right into a member of his church. Excusing himself as being ill, he hurried to his room.

The following Sunday Jerry missed church, which was often the case anyway, now that he and Betty had the twins to care for. That night Betty decided to go to church and left the twins with her parents, since Jerry said he was too tired to care for them. Later that evening, Jerry had visitors—the church member he had seen on his business trip, along with one of the church elders. Warning him that his conduct must stop, they urged him to get a job in town, where he didn't have to travel.

Ashamed of his conduct and that it was known within the church, Jerry determined to find another job and to stop his drinking. And he did find another job and he did stop his drinking, but increasingly he found excuses not to attend church. Whenever he was in church, he always wondered who knew about the encounter he had had with the church member at the hotel.

Then one evening Betty fell with one of the twins, breaking her arm and hitting the baby's head. Piling the family in the car, Jerry rushed to the local hospital emergency ward. From there, he called his sister to pick up the other baby. Later that evening, little Jeff awoke and seemed all right. However, the hospital decided to keep him overnight for observation and Betty, after having her arm set, wanted to spend the night alongside the baby.

Still worried about little Jeff, wondering how they would take care of the twins with Betty's arm in a cast, and concerned about the medical bills, Jerry passed a bar and found himself driving in. After several drinks, he drove to his sister's house to pick up little Jennifer.

When he appeared at his sister's tipsy, she refused to give him the baby. After an argument, Jerry left and ran into his brother-in-law and several church members who were returning from a church meeting.

A week later, his wife and babies okay and at home, Jerry had a visit from his pastor. It seems that the church members who had seen Jerry drunk the previous week had told the pastor and demanded that something be done about Jerry. After all, this wasn't the first time he had been seen drunk. A meeting of the deacons and church members who had seen Jerry was called. While the pastor wanted to counsel Jerry and try to get treatment for him, the church members insisted that an ultimatum be given. One more chance was all he had, then he would be excluded from the church.

When the pastor talked with Jerry and gave him the ultimatum, Jerry was extremely remorseful over his conduct and promised the pastor that it would not happen again. Encouraged to become active in church again by the pastor, Jerry did so. For the next month, Jerry was there every time the doors opened.

Then one Sunday he noticed that several people stopped talking as he approached. When this happened several times, Jerry became less eager to attend church. Three months later, he was attending only when Betty insisted that he come with her. By the end of the fourth month, he had stopped attending altogether. After a major fight with Betty about this, Jerry went out and got drunk. Church members found out about the incident, and a week later Jerry received a letter asking him not to return to church.

Soon after, Jerry started drinking on a regular basis. This was his condition when he first came to see us.

Theories of Addiction

Over the centuries, the seriousness of alcohol abuse has led to a variety of theories to account for the problem. These theories differ widely in their explanation of the root cause and in their recommendations for treatment.

The Disease Theory

Sheer willpower and rigorous self-discipline do not seem to be effective remedies for rampant addiction. In the 1950s the

American Medical Association voted approval of the disease concept of alcohol dependence. The term *disease* means "deviation from a state of health."

Some experts say that alcohol dependence is like heart disease; you are not necessarily responsible for getting the problem, but you are responsible for recovering and taking steps to avoid it in the future.

Physiologically, of course, some people are more prone to alcoholism than others, even after one drink. And often guilt drives them to more and more drinking. But then some people also have more of a struggle with greed, lust, smoking, anger, or overeating than others. Failure to contend with all of these is still sin.

The choice to use a drug as the solution to life's problems is a willful choice. And that is a sinful choice, because it is saying: "I need an alternative solution to God's way of dealing with a problem, one that will change my mood and alter my thinking immediately, no matter what the long-term effects are." Relief now is the overriding consideration.

Once that choice has been made and the drug begins to get into the system regularly, then it develops a disease state. We know now that the addiction process, especially alcoholism, acts just like any other disease. It will progress and worsen, and if untreated will eventually take a person's life.

Addiction is an interesting phenomenon. It is a willful and thus sinful *choice* that eventually becomes a *disease,* an illness. It must be treated as both. If only the illness is treated, you may cure addicts of a particular addiction, but not get to the underlying spiritual and psychological dilemmas that brought them into the addiction and may do so again. If the addiction is approached only spiritually, then you may get addicts to make some major decisions about trusting their lives to God, but the next time a stressful situation appears that they see as one "that even God can't or won't help them with," they will turn to substance abuse again and then start the disease process all over again. So the addiction must be approached from several aspects.

Alcoholism Through the Centuries

The theory that alcoholism is a disease has been around for more than two hundred years. As far as is known, it originated during the Revolutionary War in 1785, with Dr. Benjamin Rush, Surgeon General in the Continental Army (Coleman 1976). He considered alcoholism "a serious, progressive and eventually fatal disease which is incurred by the immoral behavior of the patient himself."

This concept was reaffirmed more recently by Jellinek (1960) who defined alcoholism as "a progressive and irreversible disease process characterized by loss of control over alcohol use." The loss-of-control feature is one of the prominent characteristics of alcohol abuse.

Although the medical disease model and the psychosocial learning model have both received great support in the last two to three decades, in recent history the predominant theory of alcoholism is that it is a disease. As Reinert (1968) states:

> The most popular explanation for the cause of the progression and irreversibility of alcoholism held by nonbehavioral scientists and Alcoholics Anonymous members is that there is some physiologically-based predisposition to become alcoholic. This is assumed by different students to be genetic, glandular, nutritional or allergic in nature.

Alcoholics Anonymous (AA) has adopted the disease concept. The testimonials of members who have been sober for years and have returned to a previous state of alcoholism is confirmation of their belief, "Once an alcoholic, always an alcoholic." One of Alcoholic Anonymous's official publications (1955) states:

> We alcoholics are men and women who have lost the ability to control our drinking. We know that no real alcoholic *ever* regains control. All of us felt at times that we were regaining control . . . (but) we are convinced to a man that alcoholics of our

type are in the grip of a progressive illness. Over any period of time we get worse, never better.

Was Jerry's drinking problem a disease?

To call alcoholism an illness may be confusing, since illness is technically "an interruption or perversion of function of any of the organs, an acquired morbid change in any tissue of an organism or throughout an organism, with characteristic symptoms caused by specific micro-organismal alteration" (Stedman, 1962). This technical definition of disease suggests that there is a physical cause for alcohol abuse. Numerous investigators have attempted to identify a physiological source for this "disease."

The concept of alcoholism as a disease has been controversial for years. Labeling alcoholism as a disease implies a physical, morbid process with underlying organic damage. The search for physiological variables have not been conclusive. Nutritional deficiencies or enzyme differences between alcoholics and nonalcoholics have been observed but may be *caused* by alcoholism rather than contributing to it. Alcoholism runs in families, but it is not clear whether this pattern relates more to hereditary or environmental influence. If an "addiction-prone" trait is passed genetically, the specific trait has not been identified.

The disease concept is helpful to the alcohol abuser in that it allows for medical intervention, care and supervision, but it is not helpful if it is allowed to become an excuse for behaviors and problems.

While it is undoubtedly helpful to some recovering alcoholics to see their condition as progressive and incurable, the generally accepted view of the disease concept advocates that one has to "hit bottom" before recovery can begin. This has hindered many people close to alcoholics from intervening until after the alcoholic's physical health was permanently damaged.

The Genetics Theory

The newest cause given for alcoholism and other addictions is that of genetics. According to this theory, a person is an alcoholic because it is in his or her genes to become so. An individual is driven, even doomed, by inbred makeup to be whatever his or her genes prescribe the person will be. It is as if the individual has no choice.

Was it Jerry's fate to be an alcoholic?

Not all people who agree that there is a genetic factor in alcoholism and other addictions believe it is one's fate to be or not to be an addict. However, the comments and thinking of many people involved in addiction therapy show that some, too many, do think this way.

For instance, a medical colleague recently stated that the alcoholic is no more responsible for his disease than the diabetic is for his (Wharton 1983). A similar statement from another medical colleague read that alcoholics are born (Gitlow 1983). We strongly disagree with both comments. They reflect a loss of balance in considering the causes of addiction.

When an alcoholic or an alcohol abuser learns of this theory, especially if he is a passive-dependent personality, he is likely to give in entirely to "the inevitable," to give up any attempt to try to stop, including seeking help to stop drinking. This may relieve the guilt he has from his manifested inability to stop drinking but at the same time, his self-image takes a nose dive, as he considers himself a doomed genetic "throwback" and sees himself as less than a true person.

There is reason to believe that there may be some genetic difference in many but not all alcoholics. But genetics is not the only reason individuals become alcoholics. Nor does every person with this genetic difference become an alcoholic.

The Social-Learning Theory

An alternative psychological approach to explaining alcoholism has been offered by social-learning theorists. Proponents of psychosocial learning see alcoholism as "a learned and rewarding response to problematic situations" (Hershorn,

1973). The possible rewards which could result from excessive drinking include:

1. sedative effects of a medication;
2. avoidance of participation in situations that are considered unpleasant by becoming intoxicated;
3. a social excuse for behavior otherwise considered inappropriate, such as extreme flirtation, aggression, or homosexuality;
4. the obtaining of attention through medical or psychiatric treatment from public assistance and rehabilitation programs.

Could one or more of those reasons be involved in Jerry's drinking problem?

Reduction of anxiety as a reinforcer. In humans the reduction of anxiety is an effective reinforcer as described in the experiments by Fleetwood and Diethelm (1951). They found that alcoholics produced an excess of enzymes when stressed by anxiety, tension, or resentment, and these stress enzymes were removed by adding alcohol into the blood stream. In social learning theory, the reduction of anxiety is seen as consequence conditioning, being a reinforcement for the drinking behavior.

Alcoholic behavior as a learned response. In another laboratory study of ten alcoholics and ten social drinkers (Miller et al. 1974), emotional states were demonstrated to be learned cues for drinking behavior. The experimenters asked each subject to respond to a set of verbally described social situations as they would if they really happened. In one simulated situation, the subject took his car to a service station to have a new tire put on. When he returned for the car he was told two tires were put on and the engine was tuned, which cost a total of $150.

Measures of nervous-system responsiveness indicated that both alcoholic and nonalcoholic groups were equally stressed, but the alcoholic resorted to drinking to relieve the stress more than did social drinkers. The investigators concluded that a significant part of the chain of alcohol abuse may not be the stress itself but the increased tendency by alcoholics to treat heightened emotional arousal as a cue for excessive drinking.

Reduction of cognitive dissonance as a reinforcer. The cognitive dissonance theory reasons that behavior which contradicts an important belief about oneself will arouse an uncomfortable state of psychological tension known as dissonance. In a series of three experiments, Steel, Southwick and Critchlow (1981) tested the hypothesis that among social drinkers cognitive dissonance would *increase* the amount of drinking and that this drinking in turn would *reduce* dissonance.

In the first two experiments, subjects were recruited to ostensibly make taste discriminations of alcoholic beverages. The drinking was arranged to take place immediately after dissonance was aroused from having them write an essay that was counter to their own attitudes. Students were asked to defend a position involving the university's increasing the cost of tuition. The effect of drinking on reducing dissonance was determined by measuring the subjects' attitudes immediately after the drinking task. Both experiments found that the amount of dissonance the writing project created had little effect on the quantity of alcohol consumed. However, whatever amount of drinking did occur was sufficient to reduce feelings of dissonance. This was true for both heavy and light drinkers.

The third experiment substituted coffee and water for alcoholic beverages and found that neither coffee nor water produced the dissonance-reducing change.

The practical implication of this experiment is that some forms of alcohol abuse may evolve from the reinforcement of drinking as a true means of reducing dissonance.

The social-learning concept holds that alcohol abuse is a learned response which has been reinforced by immediate, pleasant effects.

The corollary to this concept is that since alcohol abuse is learned, a behaviorally based treatment can help in learning alternative behaviors in response to conditions which previously functioned as cues to excessive drinking (Hamburg 1975).

The advocates of social-learning theory propose that the treatment goals be tailored to individual needs: abstinence for those who determine this to be the best means of control (for example, through repeated failure at controlled drinking); or controlled drinking in cases where abstinence would be more stressful than helpful, for example, a deterrent to seeking treatment (Miller & Caddy 1979; Reinert & Bowman 1968).

Social learning certainly contributes to an alcoholic's problems and behaviorally based treatment can help in that. For instance, stress can be learned as a cue not to drink but to participate in vigorous exercise—jogging, a game of racquetball, or even mopping the kitchen floor—in order to relieve the feelings of stress.

However, the social-learning theory shows little concern for what made the stress so strong that it needed immediate relief.

The Personality Theory

Another theory argued about hotly is the *personality theory,* that people with certain types of personality disorders are more likely to become addicts. (Whether or not personality traits can be called a personality disorder is a matter of degree. Everyone has personality traits that can be categorized within a certain kind of personality type. These traits become a disorder if they begin to harm our ability to function individually and with other people.)

The passive-dependent.   Most researchers and workers with alcoholics agree that the *active* alcoholic usually displays a passive-dependent (or passive-aggressive) personality disorder. However, some experts say that individuals with passive-dependent personalities are no more likely to become addicted than other personalities. Some research shows that, where results of personality tests taken before subjects became addicts have been found (naturally, these are limited in number), addicts were no more likely to have passive-dependent personalities before their alcoholism than was the population in general. And after subjects overcame their alcoholism, they did not necessarily show a strong number of passive-dependent traits either.

Despite this, through insight-oriented therapy and in-depth discussions about patients' early lives, the Minirth-Meier Clinic staff have found that the majority of their patients had strongly passive-dependent personalities *before* their addictive period began.

Such a personality is usually formed during the addict's early childhood, when he is being raised by at least one controlling parent. A second parent was often absent or inactive, as a parent, in the home. This usually involves an over-controlling mother and a father who, as far as the home is concerned, is absent, weak, or passive. (That father may exhibit much different tendencies in his job.)

More often than not, we have found that such a personality is true of the person who was the youngest child in the family, or at least the youngest child of his or her sex.

Could a passive-dependent personality be Jerry's problem, or part of it? We've already seen that he was indeed the youngest child in his family. (For a complete description of the passive-dependent personality, see the Appendix.) No one has all of these personality traits, but most addicts will have more of these than will the population in general.

Passive-dependent personalities will be dependent, clinging, helpless, indecisive (unable to make decisions); unwilling to be alone; passive in behavior in response to authority; stubborn, uncooperative, negativistic and frustrating when others ask of them; self-defeating in behavior; destructive in behavior; rude, overbearing, inconsiderate, late, careless in their work, immature; overly dependent, depressed when their needs are not met; actively aggressive only when in a position of authority or with people who cannot fight back.

Passive-dependents have a basic problem of anger or hostility; outbursts of temper; low self-esteem; an unrewarding domestic life; tenuous friendships; childish wishes; constant demands (the result of anger); little awareness that benefits must be earned and not just received; an ambivalent relationship with the mother (protective or punitive); or one parent absent or nonfunctional as a parent.

Passive-dependents look to others—usually only to one other—to give direction and to assume what should be their own responsibility. They complain to others; procrastinate; disregard instructions; avoid conforming to regulations; find loopholes; obey the letter of the law but not the spirit; contribute less than their share in relationships; nag; pout; cannot express themselves; do not say what they think or feel; cannot remember answers to questions; exhibit intentional inefficiency; want to receive more than give; feel they are not treated fairly; subtly provoke others to their own disadvantage; wait for others to come to them; feel slighted when someone disagrees with them; and give half-hearted compliance to their theological beliefs (which is also characteristic of many other church members, of course).

From the information gathered in Jerry's first interview with us, related in the beginning of this chapter, we noticed a number of his reactions fell into the passive-aggressive personality mode. We knew that Jerry would need a number of types of treatment to get over his alcoholism and to eradicate the causes that made him want to drink in the first place.

To be fair, in addition to the passive-dependent disorder, which the majority of addicts possess, we need to mention the other two personality disorders that are the largest of the minority personality disorders predominant before and after addicts' actively addictive periods. (As said previously, during *addictive* periods, addicts almost always exhibit passive-dependent disorders.)

The obsessive-compulsive.   A lot of alcoholics have hidden obsessive-compulsive, perfectionistic, traits (see the Appendix), because the same parent who is controlling and domineering usually is quite obsessive-compulsive himself or herself. By being picky with the child and expecting a lot of the child, even though the parent bails him out and teaches him irresponsibility, the pickiness produces feelings of limited, *conditional* acceptance in the child. This results in part of the child's personality wanting to please the domineering parent, although part of him also resents the parent and wants to get even.

The obsessive-compulsive is a perfectionist, who feels that anything less than perfection is reprehensible. Perfectionism produces socially disruptive sins like selfish ambition, dissension, factions, and envy (Gal. 5:19, 20). It is a factor in heart disease and other stress-related ailments. It leads to unpleasant feelings like guilt, depression, anxiety, and low self-esteem. Alcoholism becomes a coping mechanism that softens the distinction between their perfectionistic pretensions and the stubborn fact of imperfection, which is in them and all around them.

Addicts who want to please their parents more than wanting to get even with them exhibit more obsessive-compulsive traits when they recover from their alcoholism. As a result, they become independent and learn to think for themselves and often go from "rags to riches." One "town drunk," who became a Christian and then received psychotherapy at our clinic, was later elected mayor of his town.

In possibly one-third of alcoholics there are a lot of underlying obsessive-compulsive traits. The other two-thirds of recovered alcoholics function well, too, but they may not have the drive to succeed and own their own businesses or to become leaders in some other respect. They just become well-rounded good parents and mates, and good workers for other people.

The sociopath. Perhaps 10 percent of addicts are sociopathic. The sociopath is "the user." There are more and more of
these in our society today. In the last two years over 50 percent
of businessmen on polls say they would lie, cheat, or exagger-
ate on income tax returns, resumes, sales deals, and so forth,
if they knew they could get away with it. This includes many
people who call themselves Christians.

We are all born sociopaths. Satan is a pure sociopath. With
a degree of parental love and discipline, however, we change,
particularly during the teenage years. Without that we are
likely to remain sociopaths. To produce a primarily sociopathic adult personality: (1) spoil a child (two-thirds of sociopaths are from such a background); or (2) abuse a child
(probably one-third of sociopaths have experienced this background). The primarily sociopathic personality has criminal
tendencies, no conscience, feels no guilt (unless he or she gets
caught), and feels people exist only for him or her to use.

The sociopath is always manipulative. He or she makes
people feel good in order to get his or her way. Outgoing and
likeable, a sociopath makes a good "con man." There are sociopaths even in full-time Christian work.

(For more information on all three of these personality
types, see the Appendix.)

5

Putting the Parts Together

$\mathbf{M}$any people have pet theories regarding addiction, which they are able to prove—to a point. However, they all—Bible prooftext supporters, disease proponents, social-learning theorists, and personality advocates—reflect an imbalance in the cause of addiction. The various theories do not negate one another; but no one or two theories account for all the factors.

Jerry's problems, as do those of most addicts, involved (1) poor or sinful choices; (2) poor social-learning habits when under stress; (3) a personality disorder; (4) a genetic factor.

The Component of Choice

For example, the most important factor in addiction is the choice that an individual makes to take in an addictive substance to the point of excess. Many excuses have been given as to why this choice should not be considered sinful, such as not knowing where the point of excess begins, which is different for each individual. Thinking one can use a substance up to

67

that elusive point of excess but not over that point is foolhardy, and foolhardiness involves poor and sinful choices.

We don't want to pick through complex theological issues to prove the specific point where sin in substance abuse or addiction begins. That is not the issue. The fact remains that an overall wrong thinking about life leads to wrong choices which lead to addiction. Even under heavy addiction, the addict who wants to stop his habit is manifesting *an ability to choose* even if a short time later, he interrupts that choice with another one—to feel better for the moment despite the long-term results.

At the same time, we also point out that a wrong choice regarding substance abuse is no more sinful than is a choice to tell a misleading half-truth (in order to escape the consequences of telling the whole truth), nor a choice to be inconsiderate, boastful, or sarcastic (when one is overly concerned about self). Sin is sin and we are all in the boiling pot together. The difference lies only in the visible results of the sin of substance abuse, to oneself and to others. Many self-centered sins have consequences that aren't as readily traceable between cause and effect but that, nonetheless, are just as devastating to oneself and to other people.

To point out to an addict that his addiction is not only sinful but that he sinfully "brought it on himself" and that continuing to succumb to his addiction is only "giving in to sin" will not help him recover. On the contrary, it is likely to make his addiction worse. Facing his sinfulness, he may think of himself as too rotten a person to warrant God's love, anyone's love, or an addiction-free life. The addict may feel he deserves his condition. Any motivation to stop may be squelched entirely. Also the stress of facing the sinfulness of his condition may be overwhelming, and so he will look for relief from this added stress by taking in more of the substance to which he is addicted.

Pointing out that he is choosing to sin is best done slowly and carefully *after* the addict has gained control of his addiction. That an addict possesses choice in his addiction is better pointed out, first, as a positive promise of hope that he also has the innate ability to choose to accept help and take the necessary steps, however hard they may be, toward an addiction-free life.

The fact is, without the component of choice, cure would be impossible. There would be no hope. Yet addicts, when they choose to accept help medically, spiritually, and psychologically, are able to stop and become free of constantly having to fight addictive urges.

Of course many addicts stop their substance abuse through receiving help in only *one* of these areas—the medical, spiritual, or psychological. However, they often find themselves still struggling with addictive urges, if not to the strongly destructive substance to which they were once completely addicted, then to substitute addictions—food, sleep, caffeine, and other habits—many involving things that, in controlled moderation, are not only good but necessary. Uncontrolled, however, they are harmful.

Jerry *chose* to become involved in irresponsible drinking in college. He *chose* to party instead of to study. When studying, he *chose* to drink to relieve physical and psychological manifestations of anxiety. When he became a salesman, he *chose* to drink to pass the lonely and boring times he had on the road.

The Current-Stress Component

The factor of choice, however, is only one factor in the cause of addiction. It does not negate three more important components. For example, many people begin to abuse alcohol and other substances when they are under a lot of current stress. When people first begin substance abuse, it does relieve feelings of stress. Otherwise people wouldn't abuse these substances. Of course this type of relief from stress can have a terrible consequence to it later on.

Stress in no way, however, makes the factor of choice less important or more excusable, only more understandable.

The Psychological Problems
(Personality) Component

Important psychological factors come into play in sub-stance abuse and addiction which may include any or all of the issues listed below (Solomon and Patch 1974).

1. Dependency
2. Dealing with hostility
3. Relieving anxiety
4. Escape from responsibility
5. Attempting to build confidence (overcoming feelings of inferiority)
6. Regression to a more infantile state
7. Conforming to the group
8. Depression
9. Situations
10. Family structure
    (a) unhealthy communication
    (b) misuse of discipline

To ignore the above list of psychological factors would be utterly naive. On the other hand, to use them as an excuse would be irresponsible.

Note that all of these are involved in the passive-dependent personality. Jerry manifested all of them. (Compare Jerry's traits with the extended explanations of the passive-aggressive personality given in the Appendix.)

Feelings of Inferiority

While we have already discussed most of the above list of psychological issues, one that needs to be addressed is number five, that of a person's attempt to build confidence and elimi-nate feelings of inferiority.

A sense of inferiority is our most shared sense of pain. Over a long period of time, a sense of inadequacy—of falling short of the traits we believe are needed for approval—creates increasing psychological pressure from which a person eventually will seek an outlet. When a healthy outlet cannot be found, an unhealthy one will be. In today's society, that unhealthy outlet for relieving inferiority feelings is often substance abuse. Most people who are involved in substance abuse are looking for some type of relief, from current or from long-term psychological stress.

Most passive-dependent people feel inferior, that they have not been able to measure up to standards expected of their particular rung of maturity. This is because they were not taught to be independent and to make mature choices on their own. They were taught (often unconsciously by their parents) to depend on others to make hard decisions and take actions for them.

This was Jerry's problem. As the baby in a family of five children, he was always being helped out of difficult situations or protected from them by doting parents, older siblings, and teachers who succumbed to his "cute and irresistible" personality, which he had found always helped him to get his way, which usually was the easy way out.

The Biochemical (Genetic Differences) Component

The fourth important factor in addiction is the biochemical factor (Wharton 1983). Alcoholism does run in families and it has been found that those with a family history of alcoholism do develop a much higher level of acetaldehyde. In other words, some individuals simply do not metabolize alcohol as well as others. Individuals with family histories of alcoholism then are in greater danger of becoming alcoholic themselves.

Although many research projects to prove genetic differences in alcoholic families other than acetaldehyde levels have been made, their findings have not yet clearly proven a particular genetic difference or differences that could be identified before a person became alcoholic. Unfortunately, some of these research projects were undertaken and their questionable results used to try to prove that the alcoholic in an alcoholic family is blameless and cannot help his or her actions. We maintain that in such cases there were other factors at work as well.

Jerry's parents did not drink nor did his brothers or sisters abuse alcohol, but he did have grandfathers and uncles on both sides of his family who had been alcoholic. As a result, his parents were strongly against drinking. He had inherited physical tendencies toward alcoholism, and it became the ultimate in teenage rebellion for him to prove how far he could stray from his parents' standards and still, as the family "favorite," be accepted by them. Such skipping of generations in alcoholic families is not unusual.

Jerry's addiction, as do all addictions, contained multiple components. To try to cure alcoholism through one treatment method alone clearly serves only as a relief, not a cure, for the involved enormity of the problem.

6

Curing the Addict—Step-by-Step

To tell a substance-abuse addict to shape up is like telling a man who has jumped out a tenth-floor window to stop falling. An addict cannot get well without treatment—and not with one type of therapy only—but treatment in all three affected areas: the physical, mental/psychological, and the spiritual.

Curing the addict involves four different phases:

1. Identifying the problem as an addiction; intervention by those close to the addict to get him or her to admit the need for and to seek treatment
2. Detoxification, which is necessary for all but a few drugs, some of which needs to be done in a hospital environment
3. Rehabilitation in a clinical situation, sometimes as an inpatient and sometimes as an outpatient
4. Long-term follow-up, to prevent a relapse and to maintain and reinforce new patterns of sober living.

Phases of Treatment

Identification

By family members.   Not only do addicts deny that they
are suffering from an addiction but so do addicts' families. For
various reasons, family members will deny that the erratic behavior of their addicted family member, which has caused
them much grief, is truly an addiction. They blame the erratic
behavior or substance abuse (if they recognize or admit that
substance abuse is behind the behavior) on themselves for
putting too much stress on the addict or for not being all the
addict needs. Or they agree with the addict that his or her job
is too demanding or that fate, "the system," or even God, has
dealt the addict too many raw deals.

Even when they realize there is a severe problem in addition to the addict's present environment, they will usually
make excuses for the addict, rather than confronting him or
her and demanding the addict seek help. They feel sorry for
the addict, and the addict draws on that pity, manipulating
others through it, so that everyone, addict and family members alike, feel helpless. In essence, family members enable
the addict to more easily continue addictive behavior. They become the addict's enablers.

One survey showed that it was normally seven years after a
family member's problem had reached alcoholic proportions
before other members of the household were willing to admit
they were living with an addict. It took two more years for
them to seek help, for themselves or for their addicted family
member (Spickard & Thompson 1985).

By the addict.   The addict personally may agree to go for
help before he or she admits having a problem that he or she
cannot control. They may grudgingly go after being brow-
beaten by family members or even as a condition for keeping a
job, without yet admitting the seriousness of their problem.
Such addicts are poor risks for successful treatment, unless

during the treatment they admit to themselves and others that they *are* addicts and are not in control of their substance intake.

"I can stop any time I want to" usually means, "I'll never admit I want to, because I'll have to be faced with the truth that I can't." For those who are able to stop awhile, their whole thought processes often continually revolve around what they've given up. They rarely feel relaxed until they finally give in and again take in the substance they've been craving all along. Of course, the resulting feeling of relaxation and satisfaction lasts only a short time before they again begin to feel guilty and distant from loved ones, and the whole cycle of abuse is likely to begin again.

Generally, an addict seeks treatment for substance abuse upon realizing that:

1. his or her health is deteriorating.
2. he or she has lost or may lose a job.
3. his or her alibi system is beginning to fall apart. The stories made up to cover up behavior or responsibility for behavior, in order to keep the love or respect of others, no longer work.

Intervention

From the family's support base.   Family members may first attempt to seek help through the family doctor or pastor. Finally admitting their family's problem, when meeting with the doctor or pastor, they may explode in an emotional tirade of anger and tears, saying they can't take it any more and that something has to be changed immediately. While the pastor or doctor knows that nothing is going to change immediately, both can help to initiate a change in thinking of the family member and be used as referral sources for more authoritative help.

For the pastor or family doctor to use his learned caring, empathetic, and warmhearted counseling characteristics on his own, without help from others—preferably those who have personally been through the same process—means he is likely not to be believed when pointing out to family members how their actions have aided the addict in continuing the addiction. Instead of helping the family members, the pastor or doctor is more likely to end up being written off by them, and/or to be manipulated by their sad stories. This situation calls for "tough love," the concept explained by Dr. James Dobson in *Love Must Be Tough* (Dobson 1983).

An authoritative reinforcement for the pastor or family doctor could be Al-Anon, the segment of Alcoholics Anonymous devoted to family members of alcoholics, in which members of alcoholics' families meet weekly to discuss their family situations. The word of several of these people with like experiences in living with an addict, regarding the unwitting aid they provide their addicted family member, will carry much more weight than will the word of one person, albeit a pastor or family doctor, who may not have experienced personally what it's like to live with an addict in the family.

Like Alcoholics Anonymous, Al-Anon has a program that is consistent with many important Christian principles, although it is not thoroughly Christian in perspective. The basic strengths and weaknesses of Al-Anon are the same as those of AA. The speech and actions of the participants may be rougher than what some Christians feel comfortable with. However, it does include fellowship, support, and an opportunity to know that other people are suffering in a similar manner.

In some areas, through Christian counseling clinics, members of an addict's family can also be helped through individual counseling, and more likely, through Christian groups of people with like experiences.

Through Al-Anon or other such meetings, members of addicts' families begin to realize not only that there are other families that have been through what they have endured, but that, more than likely, they all have made the same mistakes of denying the problem, getting the addict out of trouble, and in other ways coddling him or her, rather than making the addict face up to the consequences of the wrongful, hurtful, and irresponsible actions he or she has displayed.

Family members who are Christians use the same types of reinforcing or enabling of the addict's problems as do non-Christian family members. However, Christians may also believe that their behavior was an attempt to follow biblical mandates of love, being their brother's keeper, or being a submissive wife.

When hearing the experiences of members of other addiction-affected families, they learn that the addict's problems are not their responsibility, that the addict should be forced to experience the consequences of his own behavior, and that family members are more victims than perpetrators of the addict's behavior.

From family members themselves.   The addict's realization of deteriorating health, the possibility of job loss, or his or her alibi system's falling apart can also come about through a planned intervention of people important in the life of the addict. The Johnson Institute in Minnesota pioneered the process of intervention with addicts. Confronting the addict all at once with a number of family members, close friends, and authorities (job supervisor, family doctor, pastor), who describe his or her unacceptable behavior in specific detail, but in a loving and nonjudgmental atmosphere, helps break down the addict's walls of denial.

If such a one-time confrontation doesn't end in an agreement by the addict to seek treatment, or if he or she agrees but continues to put it off with various excuses, then the funnel begins to tighten, individually by family members, and if needed, by another communal confrontation later on.

Each family does it differently, but an addict's family members need to begin a plan of family confrontation. Without the addict there, they need to sit down and discuss how they can slowly but steadily put pressure on their addicted family member to get into a treatment program. They must prepare to confront every form of denial imaginable. (Some addicts have been in treatment programs previously that didn't work out too well, so they will be even more calloused to the idea.)

We emphasize the need for the family to bond together in prayer warfare, praying with each other for their addicted family member. The problem that has been hush-hush between family members needs to be attacked through open prayer together.

Families need to form a funnel of loving confrontation. At the top of the funnel is the status quo—the alcoholic or addict running the show, drinking, and losing his temper, and then being sober, and the family bouncing around and recoiling to whatever he or she does. The family is not in control; the addict is. Then there is the sickening crash as he or she eventually hits bottom. To drinkers, we emphasize that "happy hour" lasts only about an hour. It is not "happy life."

Satan has had his heyday with the addict, so putting a ring of prayer around the addict and agreeing together to begin at the top of a funnel, one which will be slowly tightened with tough love, is the best approach. That tough-love approach used by the pastor or doctor with the family member of the addict now needs to be used by the family members themselves.

As this funnel progresses, the family begins to tighten in and put confrontation on the substance abuser. That confrontation might involve several procedures, which is why a professional counselor is needed to work with the family. Sometimes you may put conditions on relationships, sometimes withdrawing certain kinds of emotional support, sometimes actually distancing yourself from that person so that slowly it becomes less and less advantageous or even possible for him to abuse his addictive substance without negative consequences. As the funnel becomes tighter, the addict usually will agree to some professional help.

From business/industrial intervention programs. The identification, intervention, and treatment of alcohol abuse on the job is one of the most effective alcohol-treatment programs, in lieu of a comprehensive Christian treatment program.

Also some Christian counseling centers contract with secular businesses to provide substance abuse and other mental health therapies for employees. The spiritual part of the therapy is handled individually with each individual, depending on the person's desire for its inclusion.

In industrial alcohol programs supervisors are trained to recognize symptoms of alcohol abuse using behavioral observations. Suspected alcohol abuse is dealt with by identifying and eliminating the problems causing poor performance. Labeling the employee as alcoholic is usually avoided.

One of the major incentives that industry provides for changing behavior is the retention of one's job and source of income. The work setting is also ideal in monitoring daily performance and in providing reinforcement in job satisfaction, financial reward, and social acceptance.

Recovery rates have been reported as high as 66 percent (National Institute on Alcohol Abuse and Alcoholism 1975), making the principle of early identification and early intervention within the social system of the individual seem most appropriate (Pattison 1979). The confrontation by a significant person is considered the most efficient approach to alcohol therapy, and the work setting provides this for the person who is employed. Similar programs have also been established in military organizations.

Detoxification

Once an addict has agreed to go for treatment, a decision must be made whether he or she will be treated as an inpatient of a treatment facility or as an outpatient. Medical treatment, detoxification, is the initial therapy given. Unfortunately, some substance-abuse centers are only detoxification wards, dismissing the patient to go out and immediately start on the same cycle of substance abuse again.

Hospitals provide inpatient treatment of alcohol abuse. The major advantage of hospital programs is their ability to treat the physical complications of chronic alcoholism. Generally hospitals are more expensive and disruptive to the life of the patient and the family than are other treatment facilities. Many hospital programs have been criticized for using excessive medications, diagnostic procedures, and prolonged hospitalization. They may foster a new dependency on medications by the alcoholic (Finer 1972).

Depending on the severity of the dependency and the particular substance involved, however, hospitalization at least during the detoxification period often is a necessary and life-saving factor.

The following information gives the basic procedures followed for different types of detoxification.

Alcohol. *Intoxication* with alcohol is usually treated with observation in a protected environment. The patient is allowed to "sleep it off."

Withdrawal, however, is a different matter. Since it can be extremely dangerous, it should be done in a hospital. A complete physical, neurologic, laboratory, and psychiatric examination should be made. The patient would then receive vitamins (thiamine, folic acid, vitamin K, and vitamin C), which may help with brain encephalopathy, neuropathy, prolonged bleeding time, or scurvy. Also the patient is usually withdrawn by using a minor tranquilizer, which has cross-tolerance and will thus prevent withdrawal seizures. The patient is usually withdrawn over an approximate two-week period.

In addiction many alcoholics are dehydrated, so attention is given to fluids. Potassium and magnesium may be low and need to be supplemented. Sometimes preventive administration of antibodies is given to deal with infections. Special attention may need to be given because of fever, pulmonary infection, urinary tract infection, seizures, metabolic disturbances, hepatitis, hematolic disorders, anemia, trauma, pancreatitis, or gastrointestinal bleeding.

Barbiturates (or Similarly Acting Sedative-Hypnotic Drugs). *Intoxication* treatment for barbiturate drug abuse is like that for alcohol intoxication. Although death can result from too much overdose of the commonly used enzodiazephine (Valium), this is relatively rare. If there is any question of an overdose, however, the patient should be taken to a hospital for observation and evaluation.

Withdrawal from barbiturates is accomplished by establishing the level of tolerance with 200 mgm of phenobarbital. This short-acting barbiturate is then used to gradually withdraw the patient at the rate of 10 percent per day.

Treatment of withdrawal from a benzodiazepine (such as Valium or Librium) is by gradually decreasing the drug over a two-week period. Of course, all withdrawal should be done in a hospital, since seizures can result.

LSD.   The treatment of *bad trips* from LSD usually consists of support *(talking down)*. Benzodiazepines may be needed for sedative effects. Halopendal is sometimes used for psychotic symptoms.

PCP.   Treatment of PCP abuse and complications is controversial. Overdoses can be fatal. In general, the patient should be hospitalized and gastric suction should be administered. Urine acidification is often necessary and symptomatic medical maintenance is given. For agitation, Valium is used for control rather than antipsychotic drugs. Certainly, anticolinergeric phenothiazines are avoided. At times, Haldol is used for psychosis (inappropriate reactions to life, often including delusions and hallucinations).

Cocaine.   Cocaine withdrawal has been responsive to a number of drugs (desipramine, methylphenidate, pemoline, amantadine, and sometimes bromocriptine) and amino acids (phenylalanine, tyrosine, and tryptophan) (*Currents* April 1987).

Amphetamines.   Treatment is again given in the hospital for acute intoxication and overdose. Stimuli (such as lights and noise) are lowered. Psychotic symptoms are controlled with antipsychotics. The excretion of the drug is enhanced by acidification of the urine.

82

Opioids. *Intoxication* (acute) and overdose is treated in a hospital with a medication called Naloxone (a narcotic antagonist). Of course, support and restoration of vital functions should be attended to.

Withdrawal from heroin is accomplished with decreasing doses of oral methadone. *We are against methadone maintenance programs.* We feel the addict just substitutes one type of opioid (heroin) for another (methadone) with such therapy.

Marijuana. Some individuals on marijuana develop panic attacks, which are treated with reassurance, support, and sedatives. Some individuals develop a psychosis. These are treated with antipsychotic medication.

Tobacco and Caffeine. While most people would not include the following two categories of addiction with the life-disrupting substances considered heretofore, we must recognize that some of the addictive qualities that help trigger other types of substance abuse also tie in closely with the following substances.

Individuals have been helped in their attempts to stop smoking by gradually tapering off the number of cigarettes through behavior techniques (aversive-conditioning techniques such as the use of rubber bands), prescription gum (which helps with the withdrawal), cognitive restructuring, and self-determination.

Many individuals drink several cups of coffee, colas, and even tea, per day with resulting tremor, insomnia, and anxiety symptoms. They benefit by gradually decreasing the daily intake of caffeine.

Treatment Programs

Once detoxification has been established, the real therapy to stop the addiction is then begun. There is a wide spectrum of approaches to alcohol treatment in a variety of treatment facilities. The major systems that provide alcohol-abuse treatment programs are business and industrial alcohol programs; skid-row agencies; self-help organizations like Alcoholics

Anonymous, hospitals, mental-health clinics, community-subsidized mental-health centers and alcohol clinics.

Hospitals.   Many hospital alcohol programs incorporate participation in AA and employ "recovering" alcoholics as counselors using lectures and group sessions as part of the regimen. Some private hospitals employ aversion conditioning. In a two-week program a series of aversion conditioning treatments are given, usually by administering an emetic to induce nausea at a critical time, in order to pair the aversive response with the intake of alcoholic beverages.

The cost of the program is very high. Aversion treatment centers report success which is generally overrated. Viamontes (1972) found that only 5.8 percent of the controlled studies showed positive results. The clientele tend to be upper class, socially competent and with a strong medical orientation, and negatively disposed toward the psychological aspects of addiction.

Community-subsidized mental health centers.   The community mental-health facilities provide an alternative to hospitals that is less expensive and less disruptive. Treatment for alcohol abuse is primarily on an outpatient basis, either through individual or group therapy. When cases require detoxification and/or medical treatment, they are referred to a medical facility or inpatient program.

Alcohol clinics.   Private alcohol clinics provide similar outpatient treatment to the community mental-health centers. The cost, of course, is much higher.

The effectiveness of various treatment programs were studied by Costello (1975a, 1975b). He found that the most effective programs had a well-organized treatment philosophy that was implemented in a consistent and logical fashion; inpatient resources for medical care and nonmedical rehabilitation; an aggressive post-discharge follow-up combined with counseling and involvement with significant people in the life of the alcoholic; aggressive outreach with community activities to establish contacts and transition back into community resources, use of Antabuse as a supplemental therapy; and behaviorally oriented intervention in addition to verbal psychotherapy.

Treatment Methods

There are a variety of treatment methods that are employed by the different treatment facilities. The broad categories of methods are: psychotherapy, drug therapy, family therapy, behavior therapy, and group therapy.

Individual psychotherapy. The use of individualized psychotherapy to treat alcoholism has been addressed by several schools of psychological thought, such as transactional analysis (Steiner 1971), psychoanalysis (Hayman 1966), and eclecticism (Forrest 1975) (an interest in an array of methods which may treat different aspects of a problem). This is the school we feel coincides best with the thinking of Scripture.

The major caution of individual psychotherapy is that after detoxification, the therapist may not be aware of any current drinking, primarily among outpatients, due to the common denial and minimization of the problem among alcohol abusers. However, some clients are not suited for group therapy due to gross deficiencies in social skills and so require initial help on an individual basis.

Medical/drug therapy. A variety of pharmacological agents have been used to treat alcoholism. Some experimentation with LSD to treat alcohol addiction has had variable success but this has not had general support. The problem of addiction substitution is a major drawback and mixed-drug dependency may also develop.

An exception to this is the class of alcohol-aversion drugs. The primary alcohol-aversion drug is disulfiram (Antabuse). After taking a prescribed amount of Antabuse, the patient cannot normally drink alcohol without experiencing an averse reaction. The drug is not effective when the alcoholic is not otherwise motivated to stop drinking, but reviews of programs have shown that when Antabuse is available as a treatment option it can be a useful supplement to a multiple-treatment program.

Such drug treatment therapy by itself without other therapies in the psychological and spiritual areas is effective for only a subpopulation of alcoholics who are medically oriented and highly self-regulated. Even so, they may stop drinking but will still have responsive and addictive tendencies that are likely to cause them problems in other areas of life.

Family therapy. One of the more recent and effective therapies is the treatment of the family unit. Family problems can be seen as both a cause and consequence of substance abuse. The family environment has been shown to be a major determining factor of successful treatment outcome. The use of significant people in the life of the alcoholic to support new behaviors and relationships is proving highly successful. An extension of the family-therapy model is social-network therapy which may include such people as neighbors, friends, and co-workers.

Behavior therapy. Behavioral approaches are based on a careful analysis of the total life behavior of the alcoholic person, an application of social-learning theory. Personalized behavior techniques allow the client to determine behaviors targeted for change and to develop multiple behavioral interventions in which the patient consciously participates. Rather than considering behavior therapy as an ideological approach in itself, it is best used as part of another type of treatment.

Group therapy. Group therapy is the primary type of treatment for alcoholic patients in both inpatient and outpatient programs. In spite of wide usage and enthusiastic support by some supporters, others have challenged the effectiveness of group therapy with alcoholics. Westfield (1972) reported that only 24 percent of the inpatients who entered a program of group therapy, work therapy and recreation, or Alcoholics Anonymous, were abstinent or improved after one year. Using abstinence as a criterion for success, others report success rates of group therapy to be 25 percent (Pokorny et al.

1973) and 15 percent (Wolff 1968). In a critical appraisal of treatment methods of chronic alcoholism, Baekeland and his associates (Baekeland et al. 1975, 2:265) argued that "the evidence in favor of [group therapy] is extremely marginal." Again, we believe that is because group therapy was the only type of therapy used.

Particular problems in group therapy with alcoholics were identified (Feher 1976) as: (a) alcoholics' resistance and denial of their dependency on alcohol; (b) their tendency to define each other solely as alcoholics rather than viewing one another in a wider frame of reference as persons; (c) the variability of the alcoholic population in socioeconomic, intellectual, and educational levels, and the consequent difference in their ability to serve as constructive agents of change for each other.

The process of group therapy can deal with the first two problem areas if the group itself is functional. The critical factors appear to be the variability in group members and their ability to serve as constructive agents of change for each other. Some preliminary training on how to function as a group member is helpful in getting the group to work effectively.

Many practitioners believe that no one method has proven to be overwhelmingly successful and that the differences between patients and the particular kind of alcohol problem requires a matching of the individual to the treatment method best suited to him or her. Some studies have shown that matching patients to treatment methods can improve the outcome. Thus far the results of research have been piecemeal with several studies each adding some support.

One personality variable studied with alcoholics is the internal-external locus of control (Rotter 1966). This variable differentiates individuals on the basis of their beliefs that the outcome of their behavior is in *their* control (internal) versus the belief that the outcome is due to someone or something outside themselves—people more powerful than themselves, luck, or fate (external control). Studies have suggested that alcoholics tend to develop from those individuals who hold either of these beliefs to an extreme—the passive-aggressive with an extreme external locus of control and the obsessive-compulsive with an extreme internal locus of control, who find this thinking frustrated. The need to develop a balanced view is apparent. Some factors are within one's control; others are not.

Locus of control has been matched to treatment methods with some success in programs for anxiety, smoking modification, weight loss, and social development. Matching alcohol-abuse patients' locus of control with structure in group therapy has some potential for improving outcome.

In addition to patients' personalities, the level of involvement with alcohol is also considered. The treatment methods that are most successful for chronic alcoholics with signs of physical dependency are different from the methods which seem to work best with problem drinkers.

Withdrawal and then a single method of treatment are not enough to cure an addict long-term. Also needed are in-depth analysis of the addict's past conditioning to the world around him or her, plus opportunities to forgive and be forgiven. From our own experience, we have seen that a high ratio of success (more than 50 percent) deals primarily in using one or more therapies to correct problems in all three of an addict's life areas: physical (medical), psychological/emotional, and spiritual.

7

Curing the Whole Addict

To cure an addict comprehensively—physically, psychologically, and spiritually—all areas of the person's makeup need to be considered. The program the Minirth-Meier Clinic has employed, emphasizing the whole person and fighting the problem on various fronts—spiritually, emotionally, and physically—has resulted in keeping more than 60 percent of their patients from relapsing into substance abuse for a year or longer. In contrast, the national treatment recovery rate for alcoholism/drug addiction is much lower, even for the best programs, with a cross section showing half are drinking again in three months and as many as 80 to 90 percent are drinking again within two years (Vista Hill Foundation 1987).

The Needed Therapies

Hospitalization
While hospitalization disrupts the addict's and his family's life-style more severely, the Minirth-Meier Clinic employs

this approach to treatment for several reasons. Hospitalization treatment may take four to six weeks, with a follow-up program advised, while totally out-patient treatment may take years.

During withdrawal and detoxification, hospitalization gives the addict a protective environment in which trained professionals can detect physical complications, including the possibility of delirium tremens among severe alcoholics. Also hospitalization keeps the addict away from the temptation to continue substance use during this treatment.

Antidepressants

One-third of addicts are very depressed people. During their hospitalization, clinic patients are often treated with nonaddictive antidepressants. These help correct the depletion of serotonin and other brain chemicals that have brought on physical depression.

The temporary euphoria received from substance abuse is soon followed by pain and depression. To get rid of the pain and depression, a person must try more drugs to seek euphoria again. Sometimes the addict uses illicit drugs to relieve this pain and depression but other times he uses tranquilizers or pain killers prescribed by well-meaning physicians. In either case, as a person's system reaches tolerance, it takes more and more of the drug to experience euphoria. Eventually, no amount of the drug will bring on euphoria. The after-effect of drug-induced euphoria—depression—has become a chronic and semipermanent state, as the drug destroys more and more of the body's serotonin.

Support Systems

Finding a human support system to help addicts conquer their addiction is very important. Alcoholics Anonymous's above-average success rate is believed to be less than 50 percent although because the organization is so unstructured, no figures are available. This success rate is probably due to its support system, people helping one another. A support system provides help in sharing, caring, overcoming temptation, and direct intervention at the moment of temptation.

During hospitalization, hospital staff plus other patients in the therapy group provide this support system. Back in the community, a recovering addict needs a support system that includes not only family, but a close-knit group of exhorters and encouragers who have faced similar problems, AA or preferably a church-supported group if such is available.

Talk Therapy

A number of substance-abuse programs today are springing up that insist you don't need to use "talk" or "therapy" treatment in treating substance abuse. Part of the Minirth-Meier Clinic philosophy is that you must deal with an individual, spirit, soul, and body. Certainly the body must be dealt with and addressed. But the spiritual and psychological aspects, what we believe about ourselves and the spiritual struggles we are going through, must also be dealt with. The only way human beings take in information efficiently is through channels like talk, reading, and body language, which come under the old label of "talk therapy." These are important to reprogramming our human computers.

A teenage girl, recently committed to the clinic's care, one who had been a very compliant girl with good grades, had suddenly become involved with a punk rock group; had started taking drugs, and had left home. Apparently, her values weren't really firmly set. The counseling she is getting now is making a difference. She is being counseled about her real self and her relationship to God, herself, life, and her future. Just putting her on a withdrawal plan and sending her back into life as she was, without the counseling, would almost assure her return to drugs and drug-related friends very soon.

Many addicts from an abusive and disruptive background will outwardly appear to have a very smooth and benign image of God. But underneath they feel he is unreliable, may turn on them, and may not love them through their low times.

For addicts, initial counseling sessions often need to be spent, for quite some time, on who God is and what his nature is *really* like.

Passive-Aggressive Disorder Therapy

Many addicts have traits of a passive-aggressive personality type, and as such they often seek help first as a result of anxiety. In fact, the behavior of passive-aggressives invites stress.

A problem inherent in treatment of this personality type is that the client's behavior may antagonize the counselor. Passive-aggressive personalities do not like to be confronted openly. They tend to show up late for appointments and frequently miss counseling sessions. Out of stubbornness and habitual noncompliance, they often disregard advice given to them. After communicating a problem, they may ask for a solution. The counselor can outline positive steps for solving the problem but such clients may go out and deliberately make the solution fail, or procrastinate and not attempt to try the solution at all. Subconsciously they want to prove a therapist powerless by proving that any solutions are unworkable.

It is unwise to be directive with passive-aggressives because of their desire to prove the counselor wrong. All responsibility for a solution to a problem must be reached in an indirect or nondirective manner, allowing the counselees full responsibility for their own actions. Although individuals do not have to be passive-aggressive to show some resistance to recognizing unpleasant truths about themselves, passive-aggressives are likely to react to suggestions from others by pouting or through covertly expressed anger. Also, counselors must be extremely careful not to react to an individual's indirect aggression with direct or indirect aggression of their own.

When we work with addicts, we seldom mention drugs or alcohol, and we refuse to listen to their stories about these substances. This only encourages them to continue their habits, so they can brag about them. We also refuse to become a substitute mother. Most of them try very hard to get us to do things for them that they ought to be doing for themselves. Then they try to make us feel guilty when we refuse to do these favors for them. The best way for us to show them genuine Christian love is to be indifferent as to whether or not they like us, then to proceed to do the things that we know will have the most beneficial effects on them in the long run.

Group therapy is frequently successful with the passive-aggressive personality. Often in group therapy such individuals will become consciously aware of what they may have denied or rationalized previously. Group members will confront them when they behave too passively, and they will be encouraged to vent their true feelings and become more outgoing and spontaneous. Usually a group will react with hostility to nonverbal expressions of anger from passive-aggressives but will reward them for tactfully verbalizing their anger. This reaction effectively communicates to a passive-aggressive the effects of his or her behavior on others. However, care must be taken that the group is helpful and not rejecting.

Medication is not helpful in treating the passive-aggressive personality disorder itself. Although tranquilizers may be used to treat superimposed anxiety, dependency problems add to the risk of habituation, so regular use of potentially addicting drugs like Librium and Valium should be avoided. With passive-aggressive personalities it is best to avoid all addictive drugs. Long-term hospitalization should be used as a last resort, since it fosters dependency. Long-term outpatient psychotherapy is usually required (often for a year or more). A reality-therapy approach is recommended for this personality type. Unfortunately, even after therapy, many patients do not improve significantly because of their strong unconscious "need" or desire to fail. All passive-aggressive personality disorders can be cured if the individuals are really motivated to change and will commit themselves to persevere in the hard work of relinquishing old patterns and being transformed over time into the likeness of Christ (Rom. 12:2).

A Cure for the Long Term

The therapy the Minirth-Meier Clinic uses has never cured an addict, and it never will. The addicts who are cured through this treatment are the ones who choose to mature and to accept and effect their part in a cure; choose to work out their dependency problems; and preferably choose to switch their dependency from alcohol or drugs to God. This is not done through a one-time decision, but through holding fast to that decision as they confront their various weaknesses (a painful process), learn why they have those weaknesses, and learn how to overcome them.

Recently, a Christian phoned in to "The Minirth-Meier Clinic" daily call-in radio program to ask, "Is there a possibility that I have a disease that will make me liable to abuse drugs the rest of my life?" She is a Christian who came off drugs after a rebellious youth, stayed straight for four years, and was married. Abused by her husband, from whom she was now separated, she had started using prescription drugs, which she could get readily in her job as a nurse, to help her through her traumas. Soon, she was using drugs abusively again. Now she has been off drugs four months, but she is afraid she will have similar drug-abuse episodes the rest of her life.

Her question was a complex one because, with addiction—especially to alcohol—there is a disease aspect that brings an incredible drive to seek out the substance, once it has been introduced to a person's system. Not all of the physiology is understood, but there seem to be certain parts of the brain that react differently in those people who are driven toward consuming drugs.

However, this can be controlled by individuals who realize that they have this cyclic pattern and through taking sound, common-sense approaches to breaking that pattern. These include staying involved with health-giving and health-caring people and being involved in situations where they receive retraining and rethinking input. Christian support groups or

Alcoholics Anonymous are important parts of such a program. It is also important to stay spiritually and emotionally strong, healthy, and balanced.

In some ways, staying drug-free is like keeping something back and under control that you know can spring forth at any moment. The people who have the most trouble are those who think that when the storm clouds are past for a while and they are strong, they can drop their guard and the desire probably won't return.

We would like to see more churches begin AA-type programs, but ones that emphasize the help of the trinity—God the Father, the Son, and the Holy Spirit. The Bible says we need to exhort one another daily. The people who can best do this for former drug addicts are those who have become victorious over problems and who have gone through similar situations.

Looking at ourselves and seeing our identity in Christ as loved, accepted, and cared-for people will erase more and more of the hurts of the past.

God has given us the power of choice to live our lives to his glory or to ourselves and our own degradation. Choosing to live to his glory also means choosing to keep ourselves healthy in the physical, mental/emotional, and spiritual areas—body, soul, and spirit—of our lives.

The best alternative to drug abuse and withstanding trauma in life is balanced living:

Body—knowing and taking care of our bodies, which are houses and temples for soul and spirit—ours and God's

Soul—gaining insight into ourselves and growing in that insight

Spirit—knowing the Lord and growing in him

8

The Romans Road
to Recovery

The Minirth-Meier Clinic has adopted a twelve-stage program toward victory over addiction. This is based on scriptural principles drawn from the first fourteen chapters of the Book of Romans. (Many of these stages are similar to The Twelve Steps of Alcoholics Anonymous, which were also originally based on scriptural principles.)

Releasing addiction's hold over an individual involves uprooting psychological dependencies, identifying disease factors, and meeting spiritual needs. The addict who wants to be cured has to diligently seek insight into himself and to grow in that insight, a process made possible (and bearable) by knowing and growing in the Lord Jesus Christ (2 Peter 3:18).

During the early part of treatment, while working on the first Romans Road stages, the chemically dependent person needs to be intensely involved in withdrawing from the substance he or she abuses, (that is, becoming substance-free). This, of course, must be accomplished first in order for the substance abuser to successfully follow the program. It is a well-understood principle that addicts who continue to use drugs "in moderation" will not be able to genuinely follow through a step-type process to the point of cure.

Stage One: *Realizing that We Are All Potential Addicts* (Rom. 1:16, 21, 24)

The first stage involves an understanding of two key principles: (a) God makes no distinction between individuals; (b) we all have the potential for any addiction.

God Makes No Distinction Between Persons

Regardless of our position in life, we share the same core problem. Whether by choice, circumstance, or addiction, we have been distanced from God and find ourselves living separated and often alienated from him. All of us have only one accessible way back to God: the cross of Christ, where he died for us in order to pay the price for our journey back to him. In that regard, we are all equal. We all require the grace of God as manifested through the blood of Jesus Christ. Because of this, no one is in a position to judge anyone else. We all equally need the love and forgiveness of God.

Chemical addiction is simply one more way we can be distanced from God. At some point, every addict has experienced addiction as living in spiritual isolation, in anguish, and in separation from God. Therefore, it is crucial for the substance abuser to realize that his or her condition before God does not differ from that of any other human being. God does not categorize people as good and bad, or decent and indecent. Instead, he sees individuals as either separated and distanced from him (spiritually dead) or near to him in union and fellowship (spiritually reborn). In Romans 1:16, Paul notes that "the gospel is the power of God for the salvation of *everyone* who believes" (italics added). That power can deliver one from chemical dependence just as surely as it can deliver one from the bondage of envy, bitterness, or guilt.

We All Have the Potential for Any Addiction

Chemical dependence (addiction) is an opportunistic scourge which preys on the unwise, the unaware, and the discouraged. No one is immune to the potential for chemical addiction.

1. *The unwise* begin to dabble in occasional intoxication. In time they may dabble so extensively that they become like an individual who foolishly swims too far from shore and is swept away by the current to destruction. Lack of wisdom in early choices can later lead to tragic results when chemical dependence is involved.

2. *The unaware* don't believe in being habitually intoxicated. They use mood-altering substances (alcohol or drugs) "only moderately" and are unaware that they may have a genetic predisposition for chemical addiction. They may enter casually into the use of addictive substances, thinking they can freely walk out again later on. For many of these individuals, chemical dependence waits like a hidden trap. Although they intend to be temperate in their use of alcohol or drugs, their inherited genetic potential for addiction is there, lying dormant, waiting to be activated by their "innocent," moderate use of drugs or alcohol. Initially, they are unaware of the gradual downward spiral of the addictive process. Later they realize that they are caught hopelessly beyond their ability to free themselves from addiction.

3. *The discouraged* have turned to alcohol or drugs as a means to fill a void, a painful emptiness in their lives. This search for meaning has unfortunately taken them not toward fulfillment and the living God but toward a cruel taskmaster—addiction. Initially, the use of the substance may have been a pleasurable experience, offering relief from the

everyday pressures of life, but it was a choice to become intoxicated rather than to face the sometimes painful realities of
living.

Whatever the route, be it with the unwise, the unaware,
or the discouraged, chemical dependence is a formidable
problem. Once activated, it requires the staunchest recovery
efforts of the addict, special helpers (often including professionals), and God to overcome its power. Chemical dependence
can become a lust (craving) within a person's mind (heart)
which can totally control and destroy (defile) that individual.
(*See* Rom. 1:24.)

Stage Two: *Removing the Blinders— Admission of Our Addiction* (Rom. 2:16)

Romans 2:16 says that God will expose and judge the secrets of man through Christ Jesus. Proverbs 28:13 states that
he who conceals his shortcomings will not prosper, but he who
confesses and forsakes them will find compassion. Confessing
and forsaking involve taking full responsibility for one's current state as an addict. It is not the fault of parents, a spouse,
the community, or even God. It is the individual's responsibility. Saying that it is anyone else's fault is, in essence, passing
judgment upon another person. And judgment on another is
not allowed by God. Romans 2:1 states, "You have no excuse,
you who pass judgment on others, for when you judge another
person, you expose your own shortcomings" (paraphrase).

The blood of Jesus covers every sin and every disease we
face, but Christ did not intend to provide us with a justifica-
tion for continued irresponsibility or the use of "religious excuses," such as "The devil made me do it!" "God will forgive
me if I can't control my drinking," or "I don't need to deal with
this today; God will change me tomorrow."

Denying reality was Satan's first method for deceiving

Eve (Gen. 3:4). When Eve wanted to ignore God's command not to eat from the tree of life, Satan encouraged her to do so by denying what would be the result of such an action. He asserted, "You will not surely die." In parallel fashion, denying the reality and hard consequences of one's chemical dependence is the primary deception that keeps a person addicted. Denial is the key element in the addict's "equation of death":

$$Denial + Time = Death$$

Stage Three: *Reaffirming Our Helplessness* (Rom. 3:20)

We cannot work our way to God by good deeds, nor correspondingly can addicts work their way out of addiction by merely trying hard. Romans 3:20 states that no one by good works can in himself be justified (made right) before God. The harder we work, the more we become aware of our own inability to change into Christ's likeness. By accepting Christ, we all were forgiven by the same God and the distance between us and God was taken away; no more stigma, no more penalty.

We must still deal with the consequences of our lifestyle, however, and in the case of the addict, with the realities of his or her disease. The habit patterns and the diseases of the body (including alcoholism or any substance abuse) will continue to afflict the addict until those dependencies are dealt with. The disease of addiction attempts to ensure that addicts "fall short of the glory of God" in every way.

Whether a disease is diabetes, arthritis, alcoholism, clinical depression, or any other, all such disease processes have the potential for causing individuals to fall short of being able to fully glorify God. And yet God can be glorified in the way individuals choose to deal with a disease. When addicts admit that their lives are becoming unmanageable and that they are

powerless to resist the addiction, the process toward recovery
can begin. (The parallel principle for Stages Two and Three in
the Romans Road to Recovery is Step One in Alcoholics
Anonymous's Twelve Steps.)

Stage Four: *Recognizing the Power of Faith* (Rom. 4:17)

A physical restoration process began in Abraham with his
faith in God, as he "hoped against hope" and believed that he
could receive God's promise (of fathering nations of descen-
dants, even though his and his wife Sarah's bodies were with-
ered and old). Because of Abraham's faith, God viewed him as
capable of receiving the promise of a new beginning. Addicts
too, if they will totally believe by faith that God can restore
them, can find not only spiritual restoration and power
through a Source greater than themselves, but also emotional
and physical recovery.

Romans 4:17 states that God is "the God who gives life to
the dead and calls things that are not as though they were."
God accepts us not on the basis of anything we have done or
have failed to do, but on the basis of our faith in him and in his
power. "To the man who does not work but trusts God who jus-
tifies the wicked, his faith is credited as righteousness" (4:5).
God delights in showing himself strong in restoring the lives
of those who will not rely on their own willpower or determination, but will, with courage, place their trust totally in him.

We may have no power to overcome our own addiction, but
our faith has the ability to plug us into God's power. Our tribu-
lations may actually provide God with an opportunity to work
mightily in our lives.

The addict's "equation of life" is:

$$Tribulations + Faith = Power$$

God accepts us not on the basis of any deeds (or misdeeds)
we have done but on the basis of our absolute faith in him. The

more we, by faith, lean on him, the more he lifts us up. This is crucial if we are to believe that God can fully restore us and be our source of true hope for change.

Stage Five: *Receiving God's Unconditional Love* (Rom. 5:8, 9)

Realizing that removal of all disapproval between God and us has been accomplished in Christ enables the addict to move into a walk of faith and to activate a vital relationship with God. Paul stated that "... God's love has been released to flow into our hearts through the Holy Spirit whom he has given to us" (Rom. 5:5, paraphrase). In Romans 5, God wants us to clearly understand that, because of our faith in Jesus Christ, he is fully *for* us and not against us.

Addicts may feel that they have never had a true friend—a source of unconditional acceptance—but they now can see that a God of unconditional acceptance and love is their staunchest ally, regardless of anything in the past. They need no longer be in bondage to the disease of addiction nor fear that they are alone to resist its cruelty. Romans 5:8, 9 states, "But God demonstrates his own love for us in this: While we were still sinners [separated from God], Christ died for us. Since we have now been justified by his blood, how much more shall we be saved from God's wrath through him [Christ Jesus]." (The parallel principle to Stages Four and Five is Step Two of Alcoholics Anonymous's Twelve Steps.)

Stage Six: *Relinquishing Self-Ownership to God* (Rom. 6:13)

All individuals who put their trust in Christ can be set free from the pain of every mistake and disappointment as well as from current heartaches. Addicts can experience this, too, but they have a further need. Their pattern of alcoholism or drug addiction will continue to place them under an extending shadow of bondage unless they exercise God's power to remove that bondage from the three functions of their personality— thinking, feeling, and behavior. In Romans 6:13, Paul exhorts that you "Do not offer the parts of your body to sin as instruments of wickedness, but rather offer yourselves to God, as those who have been brought from death to life; and offer the parts of your body to him as instruments of righteousness" (KJV).

The decision to give God total rights of ownership and free reign to exercise his Lordship in each of the three major areas of one's being is difficult, especially for substance abusers who have built a life out of avoiding yielding control of any area of their lives to others. Drugs have been their sole master, and now Jesus demands that they make him Lord of their thinking, feeling, and behavior. We are not talking about a truce or a compromise with God, but about total surrender to him as Lord of every part of their lives, including those of thinking, feeling, and behavior. This decision breaks the ground for the reconstruction of addictive living patterns to begin.

Stage Seven: *Reconstructing Our Patterns of Living* (Rom. 7, 8 and 9)

Once the ground has been broken, through the addicts' decision to allow Jesus to be Lord of their lives, then reconstruction of the addictive patterns of thinking, feeling, and behaving can begin.

A. *Truthful Thinking (Rom. 7:23, 24)*

Turning over one's thinking to God comes first in this surrender. That involves realizing that we are at war in a battle against deception and denial. Paul understood this human dilemma precisely when he stated in Romans 7:23, 24, "but I see another law [or power] at work in the members of my body, waging war against the law of my *mind* and making me a prisoner of the law of sin at work within my members. What a wretched man I am! . . ." (italics added). Paul was frustrated and almost defeated at times by the internal warfare for control of his thinking processes.

The *deception* that seeks to maintain itself in addicts' lives, and through which the addiction process continues, involves *denial* of such factors as: who they really are, how and what they really feel, and what they really believe about themselves and others. If they, in self-deceit, continue to think that they are really okay in and of themselves and truly not that "sick," then they will only perpetuate the addiction. Addicts maintain a fantasy world through the defense mechanisms of denial, which allow their alcohol or drug addiction to continue. Denial is addiction's mental "friend." Addicts must face denial, allowing others to help them, if they are to break the bondage of unhealthy thinking that perpetuates their addiction. Denying that a war is being waged among the forces in the mind is deadly to an addict's chances of recovery.

B. Healthy Emotions (Rom. 8:14–16)

Turning over our feelings or emotions to the Lordship of Christ comes next. The surrender of feelings to God involves giving our deepest emotional secrets to him and requires a searching of every part of our hearts. Through the inner witness (influence) of the Holy Spirit, addicts will receive confidence and guidance to search every area of their being (Rom. 8:16). As they look into their deepest selves and conduct moral inventory, the Holy Spirit's guidance may be painful, but it is necessary. Victory over some of their deepest fears can be accomplished at this point.

The deepest fear faced by all addicts is that, if they should leave their "mistress of addiction" and cling instead to God, he may forsake them when he sees them without the camouflage of their substance abuse. After all, substance abusers

have feared rejection for years, enough so that they learned to
make the avoiding of transparency a habit. Manipulation
and deception have been their means of survival for years.
Their bondage (slavery) to the fear of rejection is referred to
in Romans 8:16 as "a spirit of slavery leading to fear again."

God is our good Father, however, to whom we can tell every
secret within our hearts without fear. Regardless of how sor-
did, painful and deep our moral inventory and emotional dis-
closure become, however, Paul teaches us (Rom. 8:38, 39) that
it will not separate us from God's love. Hiding ourselves from
God through deception and avoidance are no longer necessary
when we are convinced, like Paul, ". . . that neither death nor
life, neither angels nor demons, neither the present nor the future, nor any powers, neither height nor depth nor anything
else in all creation, will be able to separate us from the love of
God that is in Christ Jesus our LORD."

C. Responsible Behavior (Rom. 9:20, 21)

Turning over one's behavior (or actions) totally to God is the
third specific step of surrender addicts must make, after they
relinquish their thinking and emotions in detail to him.
Surrender of actions involves allowing God to deal with every
behavioral pattern, flaw, and point of vulnerability in our
character; to scrutinize every motive; and to "coach" every
action. Paul states that life's outcome does not depend on individuals who use their will to run life's race; it is God's mercy
instead that gives the victory (v. 16). To be sure, addicts must
make themselves totally *available* for this race, but it is his
power that will accomplish the changing.

Verses 20 and 21 of Romans 9 describe us all as clay in the
Potter's hands. Only the Potter, not the clay itself, has the ability to make a beautiful and useful object from the clay. Addicts
must believe that, if they surrender fully to God, he will mold
them into a vessel for his glory, "fit for the Master's use." Such
a vessel must desire to be ultimately free of any flaw, including that of chemical dependency.

Key milestones in this third step toward complete surrender include:

Independence

The first milestone to learning more appropriate behavior begins with part of our first step of surrender—changed *thinking*—and involves grasping the concept of independence. Chemically dependent individuals habitually depend on others to make decisions for them, a process which often begins in childhood. Now they must learn to make their own decisions. They can no longer turn to others to make decisions for them or to substance abuse to blur reality for them.

Self-Concept

The second milestone involves changing one's self-concept, a part of changed *feelings*. This helps addicts to learn to like or appreciate themselves in Christ and assists them in gaining confidence as they diffuse guilt and experience successes in behaviors. (See Don Hawkins' *Your Self-Concept,* an Acorn booklet from Moody Press, 1987.) The guilt has come from hurting others in the past, failing to live up to the expectations of others, or from being excessively needy and dependent on other people. Left unresolved, the guilt can and will continue to destroy relationships and perpetuate addiction if it is not dealt with along the road toward improving the addict's self-concept.

Self-Discipline

While practicing decision-making, under progressively more demanding circumstances, addicts reach the third milestone toward living out their surrender to God, a major part of changed *behavior*. It involves learning to refuse the "easy way out" of painful situations. An individual at this stage begins to take personal responsibility for changes, rather than just being told to make them. This is rewarding to see.

God sets a standard for us that is higher than we would ever set for ourselves. And yet He promises that we have the potential to meet that standard when we follow through on the initial surrender of our entire being. We do this by allowing him to work his power through us day by day and step by step in the process of reconstructing our patterns of thinking, feeling, and behavior. (The parallel principle for Stage Seven in the Romans Road to Recovery is Step Four of Alcoholics Anonymous's Twelve Steps.)

Stage Eight: *Rounding Out the Intensive Internal Audit* (Rom. 10:9–11)

At this point, a deep self-search is undertaken as addicts review earlier stages. Often a fear emerges that they will feel disappointed and empty with what remains in their lives after they give up their deepest grievances, indulgences, self-concessions, and beliefs about themselves. As miserable as their lives often have been, they were at least lives that they understood. They must rigorously search the "hidden closets" of their minds to identify as many of those secret thoughts and beliefs as they can, as well as the fears and inner frustrations that were involved in keeping such thoughts, beliefs, and memories hidden deep within.

As ironic as it might seem, a grieving process now begins when the addicts see themselves meeting head-on the need to let go entirely of a "trusted" old friend, a constant companion they know well—the addiction. They need to allow themselves to experience this grieving process fully, if they are to continue stepping away from their addiction. This process of grieving needs to cover the addictive lifestyle in its totality—memories, experiences, and sometimes even friends.

Resolving the grief comes when recovering addicts look to a future with God that will not disappoint them, but will truly fulfill them. "No one who believes in Christ will ever be disappointed" (Rom. 10:11, LIVING).

This is also a time for addicts to renew their vows to God and to remember how he brought them into salvation and fellowship with him. "If you confess with your mouth that Jesus is Lord, and believe in your heart that God has raised him from the dead, you will be saved" (Rom. 10:9).

At this point, it is crucial to the addicts' recovery for them to believe that their deepest fears have been replaced with hope, to remember that the wonderful gift of salvation through Jesus Christ is theirs, and to realize that his promises will never disappoint them. (The parallel principles to Stage Eight in the Romans Road to Recovery are Steps Five, Six, and Seven of Alcoholic Anonymous's Twelve Steps.)

Stage Nine: *Restoring Broken Relationships* (Rom. 11:22, 23)

A solid focus not on self but on others—especially on those whom addicts have wronged, hurt, or considered enemies in the past—is crucial at this juncture. Romans 11 is a chapter on reconciliation and of bringing about an attitude of restoration through relationships. That must occur in the addicts' lives if they are to see themselves not only as beloved by God but responsible for acting in love toward others.

In Romans 11:22, the nation Israel is told to show God's kindness and to grow in God's likeness if the nation wants God to continue his favor toward her. This verse also applies to all Christians, but addicts in particular deeply sense a need at this point to extend to others the love and favor God has shown them. God feels strongly about forgiveness of others. He also desires to rebuild broken relationships. In the Scriptures, God often uses the Jewish nation to illustrate how relationships that have been cut off in the past can be grafted back, in order to become alive and fruitful once again (11:23).

Whenever possible this may involve going to others, admitting wrongdoings, and correcting and making amends. Such bridge building leads to continued progress toward recovery. An individual who will not deal with bitterness or grievances toward others will lose the capacity to remain intimate with God. He or she will eventually slide back through these stages toward substance bondage once again.

Intimacy is a key factor in restoring relationships. Essentially it is an emotional and behavioral commitment to be open with other people, to give and receive help from others, and not to be judgmental or manipulative in the process. Healthy interactions with family, especially in intensive family-therapy sessions, will promote the uncovering and healing of both spousal and parent/child conflicts.

As the addict's ability to develop intimate relationships in general improves, a strong basis is provided for correcting previously damaged relationships. As these relationships are restored, insight into the way other individuals think and behave is often deepened. This is especially helpful in identifying, understanding, and resolving feelings and attitudes that affected others negatively. (The parallel principle for Stage Nine in the Romans Road to Recovery are Steps Eight and Nine in Alcoholic Anonymous's Twelve Steps.)

Stage Ten: *Replacing One's Lifestyle* (Rom. 12:1, 2, 9)

Renewing one's mind, giving one's life day by day to Christ's total Lordship and control, and loving him without hypocrisy are the goals of this level. Addicts must continue regularly to both believe and act on the basis of a new self-definition of being slaves now not to chemical dependency but to Jesus Christ. At this point, addicts must continue to work on restoring key family and social relationships that were damaged or lost due to the substance abuse.

An element of enormous importance now is *repetition,* prac-

ticing again and again, in total submission to the will of
Christ, the implementing of new, healthier thought processes,
feelings, and behaviors. These are the building blocks for the
addict's new lifestyle of responsible, drug-free living. Addicts
must learn to face and admit mistakes promptly, to avoid denial at all costs, and to be willing to be painfully transparent
on a daily basis. In Luke 9:23, Christ stated that we must take
up our cross daily and follow him. Addicts must continue to
practice these new, healthier ways of living until they see
them not as just "second nature" but as their "new nature."
(The parallel principle for Stage Ten in the Romans Road to
Recovery are Steps Ten and Eleven in Alcoholics Anonymous's
Twelve Steps.)

Stage Eleven: *Relieving Others'*
Burdens
(Rom. 13:9, 10)

Concentrating on kindness toward others, being willing to
serve and to love them in a Christlike fashion, is involved in
this stage. The wisdom and personal maturity attained at this
stage will prepare the addict for the final step of the renewal
process, which is taking the message of redemption and recovery to others.

In order to be prepared to take this message to others, recovering addicts must be well grounded in the practices of
kindness and compassion that Scripture calls on us to show
toward others. In the past, addicts' lives were centered so much
on their own problems that they hardly knew the specifics of
how to show love and compassion to people. They were spiritually near-sighted, unable to *see* the needs of others much less
to *meet* those needs. In Romans 13:9, 10 Paul states, " 'Love
your neighbor as yourself.' Love does no harm to its neighbor.
Therefore love is the fulfillment of the law."

When addicts keep a clear conscience and are willing to be
transparent and honest enough to "owe nothing to anyone, ex-

cept the love of a clear conscience" (v. 8, paraphrase), then they will be able to continually draw closer to God. James 1:5 promises that God will give wisdom to those who ask for it. As recovering addicts seek to improve their conscious contact with God through prayer and meditation, they must continually ask him for his insight and guidance.

Conversely, Proverbs 28:9, 14 warns that God will turn his ear away from us if we no longer seek to obey him. He will also allow calamity to come to those who harden their hearts toward him. God is intensely interested in establishing and maintaining an intimate relationship with all his children, and this certainly applies to the substance abuser. Like a good father who knows what is best for his children, God will discipline us if we stray from a close relationship with him. And yet he will also bring us back into loving fellowship with him time and time again. We crucially need not only to enjoy this fellowship and compassion with the Lord ourselves, but also to be willing to extend it to others.

Stage Twelve: *Reaching Out to Others* (Rom. 14:15-17)

The goal of every Christian is to reach out to others to bring them into the process of redemption, renewal, and realization of a full and healthy life in Jesus Christ. This especially should be the goal of recovered substance abusers. Romans 14:15-17 states that we are to live life so as not to lead others into any form of bondage, either of emotional bitterness or of chemical dependency. We are not to be stumbling blocks for our brothers but witnesses for Christ in their lives. So we shine as examples of what God can do in a human being to effect not only redemption from sin but also recovery from the disease of addiction. Romans 15:1, 2 explains that we are to bear the weaknesses of others with our strength and not just please ourselves. We are to see others through the eyes of Christ and attain a position of productive service to the Lord.

As addicts realize the miraculous changes that God has brought to their lives, they are enabled to unselfishly serve others and reach out to them. As they experience the love and newness of life that Christ has brought and the freedom from chemical dependency, which by now has become a real possession and not just a dream, they begin to see others being drawn to them because of the newfound meaning to their lives. The ultimate "high" for formerly chemically dependent Christians is to see themselves being used regularly by God as vessels for communicating healing to others, as they go forward with the promise that "the God of all hope fill you with all joy and peace that you may abound in hope by the power of the Holy Spirit" (15:13). (The parallel principle for Stage Twelve in the Romans Road to Recovery is Step Twelve in Alcoholic Anonymous's Twelve Steps.)

9

Abusers and Their Families

When addicts are cured of substance abuse, sometimes the battle is just beginning for their loved ones. They need therapy just as badly as their substance-abusing family members. Without it, once their addiction-prone relative is cured, they are likely to face and cope poorly with the need for healing their own deep emotional scars.

Sarah and Sam

Four years after Sam's conversion to Christ and recovery from alcoholism, Sarah, his long-suffering Christian wife, came to us, now a drug addict and suicidal herself. When Sam was cured, no one had helped Sarah learn how to cope with a well husband.

Sarah used to go to Wednesday-night prayer meeting and tell others how she was suffering for Jesus, and ask prayer for her husband. Church members were impressed with Sarah's fortitude in this situation. She rarely seemed depressed.

Sarah's attitude was not because of some superspirituality,

however. It was as though Sarah *delighted* in suffering, as if it was her purpose for living. She had suffered all her life. Her alcoholic father had been unfaithful to her mother and had sexually abused Sarah. Since her father was away most of the time, she had craved his affection, despite the sexual abuse. As a result, she developed hysterical personality traits— craving other people's attention, particularly that of the opposite sex who would remind her of her father. Like many children of alcoholics, she had married someone who would keep her in the alcoholic-family system that she was used to.

When Sam became a Christian, overcame his alcoholism, and became a successful businessman, Sarah began to fall apart. She was uncomfortable with having a nice, loving husband. Wanting to leave him and not knowing why, she became increasingly depressed.

Having been the family breadwinner, as well as primary parent and disciplinarian, she fought Sam's attempts to take over some of the roles she had taken on. The more responsibility he assumed, the more worthless Sarah felt herself to be. The more her children showed a new love for him, the less loved she felt. As she saw it, she wasn't needed or loved as much anymore by her children or her husband.

Sarah didn't know how to relate to a successful husband. All the men in her life, including her father, had been losers. Early in life she had determined that her job was to rescue losers, but unconsciously she didn't try to rescue them completely, because she needed to feel needed as their rescuer in the future, as well. *She was addicted to enabling addicts.*

Sarah's new situation created feelings of anxiety in her, but she didn't know why. Soon she couldn't sleep at night. Her family doctor prescribed a limited amount of Darvon to help her relax. She felt much better when taking the drug, but the uneasy feelings continued to grow when she did not take it. When her doctor refused to renew her prescription, she went to another doctor who did, and then to another and another, in order to have an endless supply of the prescription on hand. Soon she was addicted to Darvon.

Even though she had been a great opposer of alcohol, Sarah also started drinking to escape her feelings of confusion and anger. Eventually she began stopping off at a bar for a drink, where she would talk to men who were alcoholics, men for whom she could feel needed. Later this former "suffering saint" started dating other alcoholics, and within a few years found herself to be alcoholic too.

Ironically, Sam now found himself in reverse roles with Sarah. Sarah eventually reached such a level of drug and alcohol dependence that she was hospitalized after an overdose of Darvon.

Although Sarah wanted help to overcome this situation, while she was in the hospital she developed a crush on an alcoholic patient and tried to have an affair with him. She desperately wanted to divorce her good husband and marry another alcoholic—one who would be unfaithful—because that was what she had been used to all her life, and what she felt was her reason for living. She somehow equated that with "suffering for Jesus."

Through three months of hospitalization therapy, Sarah began to realize her masochism, saw her childhood emotional scars healed, and began changing into a healthy, happy Christian woman. In the years since her hospitalization, she and Sam have had a few ups and down, but overall they have done very well. They continue to progress through the normal maturing process that marriage is meant to provide.

The Need for Family Therapy

Believe it or not, Sarah's case is not unusual. It is all too typical of what can happen when a substance abuser changes lifestyles and no insightful help or therapy is given to family members to help them change their own outlook on and purpose for living.

We have treated many alcoholics through our clinic and have found that not only do alcoholics need therapy for personal growth, but so do their mates, and sometimes even their children. As we mentioned earlier, when alcoholics recover from their alcohol problems and begin to really enjoy life without alcohol, initially their mates will have a more difficult time adjusting to this success than they did to the former substance abuse! Change is often frightening, even when it is change for the better.

From Individual Therapy to Family Therapy

Drug or alcohol abuse has commonly been regarded as a problem inside the individual, a result of inherited genes or of poor learning from early-life experiences. In this thinking, the consequence is that the individual possessed a weakness which resulted in substance abuse. Such thinking creates an orientation that focused on making only the abuser responsible for change.

A shift in thinking has now emerged in the context of family therapy. While the individual is still responsible, the addict or abuser is seen to be in the context of a family system, and change in the person also requires a reciprocal change in the family system.

The family is the smallest social unit, and we believe is God's ordained pattern for teaching about society's demands and for passing on values. The law of Moses stated this specifically.

> These commandments that I give you today are to be upon your hearts. Impress them on your children. Talk about them when you sit at home and when you walk along the road, when you lie down and when you get up.
>
> Deut. 6:6, 7

The family then is the primary social unit for learning relationships, roles, and patterns of interaction.

Family Subsystems

The nuclear family has been described by Minuchin (1979) as having at least three subsystems: parental, spousal, and sibling. When a mother tells her young son to drink his milk and he obeys, mother and child are building a pattern that has far-reaching consequences. A hierarchy is being established, which includes respect for the superior knowledge and wisdom of the parent. Trust is developed in the mother's care when the milk tastes good, and over the long run proves to be good for the child's health. A mother has to act like a mother so that the son can act like a son, and vice versa.

The *spousal system* is an arena of complementarity, of learning how to give to each other without feeling that one has given up anything. Such a relationship is described in Ephesians 5:21-23, 25.

> Submit to one another out of reverence for Christ. Wives, submit to your husbands as to the LORD. For the husband is the head of the wife as Christ is the head of the church, his body, of which he is the Savior. . . . Husbands, love your wives, just as Christ loved the church and gave himself up for her.

In the *parental subsystem,* parents and children negotiate decisions from positions of inequal power.

> Children, obey your parents in the LORD, for this is right. "Honor your father and mother"—which is the first commandment with a promise—"that it may go well with you and that you may enjoy long life on the earth."
>
> Fathers, do not exasperate your children; instead, bring them up in the training and instruction of the LORD.
>
> Eph. 6:1–4

> When I was a child, I talked like a child, I thought like a child, I reasoned like a child. When I became a man, I put childish ways behind me.
>
> 1 Cor. 13:11

In the *sibling subsystem,* children interact more as peers, negotiating issues of competition, defeat, accommodation, cooperation, and protection.

> Contend, O LORD, with those who contend with me;
> fight against those who fight against me.
>
> Ps. 35:1

> How good and pleasant it is when brothers live
> together in unity!
>
> Ps. 133:1

When these subsystems are not functioning or are interacting in ways that hurt rather than help family members cope with life stresses, drug or alcohol abuse may develop. In many cases, it is often difficult to tell whether substance abuse is a cause or an effect of family problems.

Similarities in Families of Substance Abuse

There are striking similarities in families of drug dependents and alcoholics. Dr. Ziegler-Drisscoll (1979) reported on family studies which compared ninety families with alcoholic and drug-dependent members. The percentage of relatives who abuse substances (primarily alcohol) of the patients in treatment is given below:

Type Patient	Patients with Substance-Abusing Relatives	Fathers	Mothers	Other Relatives
Drug dependent	63%	39%	7%	22%
Alcoholic	68%	39%	7%	64%

It can be seen that very little difference is evident between the families of drug-dependent patients and the families of alcoholics. The prominence of the father's substance abuse is equal in both families.

It was found that families of substance abusers had three things in common.

1. They *lacked understanding about addiction* and the role it played in the life of the abuser *and tended to react inappropriately* to the problem.

2. There was an *overly dependent relationship* among younger substance abusers with one of the parents. Separation from parental involvement was one of the important adolescent tasks which had not been resolved. The abuser had been spoiled or overprotected as they were growing up.

3. In more than 64 percent of the families *the father was either absent or a peripheral figure*. In some cases, where the father was present, he had relegated major responsibility for child rearing to his spouse. In single-parent families, when the child had taken on the responsibilities of the missing parent and missed the experiences of adolescence, later substance abuse may have appeared as a way of getting out from under responsibilities which came too soon and were too burdensome.

Keeping the Sick Family Sick

Substance abuse by a family member can be understood as a symptom of a malfunctioning family. To understand drug or alcohol abuse, one should consider how all family members contribute to make the addictive behavior of one member possible and how that behavior affects each individual in the family system.

Homeostasis is a concept introduced in family therapy by Don Jackson (1957). According to this concept, family members work at keeping the family system in balance; they have built-in mechanisms to resist change. Whenever events impact on the family to offset the way members relate to each other, the members shift as necessary to restore a balance.

Part of the stabilizing pattern may include drug or alcohol abuse. In this context, to change the substance-abuse behavior of one member is not enough to help the family conquer its basic problems. In fact, it can even cause other family problems to get out of control. Clinical evidence now suggests that abstinence as an isolated change often increases pressure on other family members and on family interaction, including dissolution of the marriage.

After a family member's recovery from addiction, the other family members, in particular the spouse, may either (1) fall apart; (2) drag the recovered addict back into his or her addiction, in order to keep the system or life-style going that he or she had become used to and felt most comfortable in coping with; or (3) become estranged from the former addict.

This is especially true if the spouse comes from an addictive and abusive family system as a child. And many spouses of addicts do come from such backgrounds, as did Sarah, the wife of the recovered alcoholic who became a drug addict herself.

Ralph and Shirley

One such case was Ralph and his wife, Shirley. Ralph was a recovering alcoholic who, after ten years of abusive drinking, was sober for eight months prior to coming in for marital counseling. He was attending Alcoholics Anonymous meetings faithfully three to five times a week. His boss at work was supportive and continually encouraged him.

Shirley had learned to cope with Ralph's drinking and had joined a support group for wives of alcoholics. She had become a popular speaker for her group and had gained status and self-esteem from her public-speaking engagements. For years her husband's alcoholic behavior provided a wealth of anecdotal material, and she was exceptionally good at using her tales to convince audiences she understood and could identify with every abuse an alcoholic could inflict on his family.

But now that Ralph was sober, this was more difficult. Shirley candidly admitted in therapy that her life was better when Ralph was drinking. In fact, since he had become sober, Shirley had tried to induce Ralph to drink in not too subtle ways. She threw drinking parties for family and friends who were known for their abusive drinking patterns. She kept a good supply of alcohol in the house and increased her drinking in Ralph's presence. She resisted changes in the marriage and sabotaged efforts which enhanced their relationship, during the week as well as in the therapy session. It became obvious that Shirley was desperately trying to keep the family sick so she could capitalize on its pathology in her specialized speaker's role. A year later, Ralph was maintaining sobriety—a difficult task under circumstances that would have driven many cured addicts back to active addiction—and Shirley had filed for divorce.

While Shirley's case was special, considering her "speaking career," many other spouses of addicts have learned to depend on their role as the "suffering spouse" to gain needed approval and sympathy from outsiders.

The Needs of Teenage Addicts' Families

Until the 1940s and 1950s, psychotherapy was considered primarily a practice aimed at individuals and their problems only. Then therapists working with schizophrenic children "discovered" that these children had parents. The relationship between the two generations, they began to realize, strongly affected schizophrenic children's psychiatric problems. As a result, family therapy became a much-expanded field.

Not until a much later date, the early 1970s, did some therapists and other health workers involved with alcoholics and drug addicts begin to be aware that addicts too have parents, and that the previous generation has much to do with present addicts' problems. Even when addicts are grown and have established homes of their own, and even if their parents are no longer living, still their parental upbringing and those early interactions live on inside them. We often see one dominant parent who controls the family either through emotional, verbal, physical, or guilt intimidation.

Dottie, a drug addict, who was very attractive, came from a wealthy Christian home. A Christian herself, Dottie had gone to church all of her life and had attended a good Christian camp every summer for seven years. She would often re-dedicate her life to God.

Dottie's parents were so dominant, however, that she felt little self-worth because of her dependency on her parents, who had never encouraged her to make decisions and do things for herself. As a result, because of peer pressure, she soon succumbed to the other kids' teasing about her refusal to try marijuana or alcohol.

In fact, Dottie tended to yield to the values of whatever group she was in. If she was with a group of Christians, she was a model Christian. If she was with those who desired drugs or alcohol, she became one of them. This was in spite of her desire to live for Christ. Dottie did this because she was weak—*passive-dependent*—dependent on pleasing her parents in order to gain strength and self-worth, which she now carried over to pleasing her peers. Her parents had never encouraged her to form opinions other than theirs.

Besides insight-oriented therapy, we taught her to be more responsible and independent in appropriate ways. We gave in-directive therapy (helping her to decide for herself what she ought to do, rather than telling her what to do); guided her with Scripture in how to make correct choices; and provided family therapy for her family.

Two other alcoholic teenagers, admitted at the same time, received the same treatment approach. Although their parents were not Christians, they cooperated fairly well in the program, and both of their daughters did well when they were released. Dottie, the drug addict, on the other hand, did not do as well. Once she was released from the hospital, her Christian family did not cooperate well in her outpatient therapy. They were wealthy, used to doing things their own way, and continued to be critical of her and to think for her when she returned home.

Even though Dottie was over her drug addiction when she left the hospital, about two or three months later she was addicted to drugs again, driven there by her parents' overcontrol and criticalness. She refused to come back for therapy, even though we strongly recommended to her that she do so. The family, rather than acknowledging that they had any responsibility for her downfall, decided to put her in another type of drug program that treats addicts with medication only and doesn't get into "talk"—family and insight-oriented— therapy. They did not want to acknowledge their part in her problem. They were not facing the fact that drug abuse is a people problem as well as a chemical problem.

The best thing parents can do for addicts, teenage or adult, is to help them become aware that they are loved and yet insist that they take the initiative to assume responsibility for their own decisions and behaviors. Such parents through tough love need to refuse to do things for their passive, addictive children, even if it means the children fall on their faces several times before realizing that they and they alone are responsible for getting things done in their lives. It is not helpful to shield the addict from the consequences of his or her actions.

We encourage parents not to give addict sons and daughters money. That just supports their habit. And we tell parents not to get them out of trouble with the law. They desperately need to experience the consequences of their own behavior, since they often did not when they were growing up.

We quote Dr. Paul Meier, who is fond of vividly and exaggeratingly making a point. "I think the ideal treatment for an alcoholic or drug addict would be to send him or her into a remote jungle for a month or two with a Bible, a compass, and a jackknife, with nobody around for several hundred miles, especially the addict's mother. This would produce independence, maturity, and increased self-confidence, and I'm sure would cure many addicts of their passive-dependent personality disorder."

Such a cure is probably not as easy as that, but we would all agree that learning to fully accept responsibility for one's own recovery is essential to the success of an addict's treatment.

Children of Alcoholics

Not only do spouses and parents of alcoholics need special help, but so do alcoholics' children. Otherwise, many children of alcoholics are also likely to become alcoholic, or become spouses of alcoholics, or become fierce, zealous teetotalers, whose own children are likely to become addicts or at best lead lives punctuated in adulthood by feelings of self-doubt and emotional insecurity.

Those Who Marry Back into the System

Children of alcoholics often tend to marry alcoholics or those people who have all the tendencies of approaching alcoholism. There are a number of reasons for this.

To replay and correct their childhood.   One reason is that such a marriage allows the child of alcoholics to attempt to replay and correct their own childhood this time around. In some ways, the person feels they can go back and undo the past, as if the parents' addiction were their fault. It is like the college athlete who blew it royally in an important game years ago who continually talks about how he would replay that game next time, if given the chance.

To rescue an alcoholic.   Another reason for such a marriage is the desire left over from childhood to rescue the addictive parent. Many times a child saw an addictive parent struggling and felt helpless to solve the situation, so they married an alcoholic whom they feel, now as an adult, they can rescue. Somehow they feel this will give them a sense of self-worth, which was robbed from them as a child when they felt so helpless.

To repent of lack of childhood spirituality.   A third reason, which is a little deeper and more unusual, is as a form of penance, almost a way of saying, "I'm sorry I was bad (which I must have been since I was abused in an alcoholic home). This time," they think, "I'll be a better helper to my alcoholic loved one than I was the last time." With a warped sense of theology, they seem to assume that God will then think more of them.

Those Who Turn Out Well

Of course, many children from alcoholic homes grow up better than might be expected. If you talk to people in churches, you will find that a fair percentage of active church members grew up in homes that were experiencing active alcoholism or had an alcoholism problem with an aunt, uncle, or grandparent.

Even when such children do turn out well, however, it is not without great stress in the past and present. Their background has produced a sense of uncertainty in life, because the parent's mental state and the well-being of the home was always subject to change at any point. If Dad went on an alcoholic binge, or if he began drinking heavily for a period of two or three months, he may have come home and been very violent. He may have been emotionally very supportive, nurturing, and easily approached one day and the next day have been intoxicated and appear just the opposite.

If Dad was drinking for several months and there was a deterioration in his function, there may have been a job loss. Some of these children were never sure when they started school in September that they would finish the school term in May at the same school. Dad may have lost his job, been asked or forced to leave the community because of legal problems, and so forth. It is usually Dad but not always.

Those Who Adopt Certain Roles

Children of alcoholics have to go through some difficult and stressful processes to survive. They see childhood as something to be survived, rarely something to be enjoyed and feel nurtured in. To survive, they often play different roles.

The scapegoat. This child will become the negative achiever in the family, the one who seeks negative attention. He or she thinks, "If I can be more of a problem than the drug abuser, then maybe I can get the attention that I need." It is a negative use of the adage "the squeaky wheel gets the oil."

The family hero. Family heroes take the opposite approach. Perhaps by being the best child, the most loving youngster, one who makes the best grades and is the finest soccer player, then by being a superachiever, such children feel they can somehow draw the family out of its addiction. "Maybe if Dad had the best son in the world, he wouldn't need the alcohol." "Maybe if Mom had the best little girl that God had ever created, she could love me enough that she wouldn't need that alcohol that she drinks."

The lost child. These children are the ones who can't muster the grit to be the scapegoat and perhaps they can't achieve enough to be the family hero. So they just go with the flow and are very passive. They are the ones who are very likely to become victims of substance abuse themselves. They decide the best defense is to become invisible. If they could just dissolve into the wall, they would. They don't like to be picked out as either good or bad. They just want to be nonentities. "If I'm not here, maybe that will cool down the situation. Besides, if I'm not here, it won't be as painful."

The clown. Many entertainers, some of the most popular comedians in the country, have alcoholic-parent backgrounds. They become the clown. If they can divert attention from the seriousness of the problem and be a clown, they sometimes see that they can diffuse the anxiety and pain and help overcome their own feelings of pain. They become jokesters and pranksters. You see them in every church, the guys who can't say two serious words. Many times they come from homes where there is a lot of pain.

Those Whose Children Become Alcoholic

Teetotaling children of alcoholics are much more likely to keep their own children from abusing alcohol by educating themselves and then educating their children in the various aspects of and outlooks on alcohol, rather than by merely pronouncing a family edict against alcohol and emotionally ranting about its evils. Teenagers and young adults need reasoned and knowledgeable evidence for the parental viewpoint and opportunities to discuss the various pros and cons other people (including medical doctors) use for controlled drinking.

Without that it isn't likely that teenagers or young adults will develop the personal defenses they need to choose not to drink in the face of outer and inner temptations they will meet to use alcohol socially and even abusively. They may see their parents' very emotional reactions to alcohol (formed from the parents' stressful childhoods, to which the children cannot relate) as totally unreasonable.

Those Who Are Being Transformed

Children of alcoholics carry the marks of their childhood with them into adulthood. And those who adopt any one of these four childhood roles—the clown, the family hero, the scapegoat, and the lost child—will carry those roles with them throughout the entirety of their lives. Of course, those can be modified and brought under the subjection of Christ and the Holy Spirit, but it takes a lot of effort, time, and insight.

Of course, all children—those from alcoholic families or not—have problems they need to bring under the restructuring power of the Holy Spirit. None of us had perfect childhood backgrounds. As the Bible says, we are to be transformed through the renewing of our minds (Rom. 12:2). And in many ways this transforming involves going back and undoing some of the negative emotions, outlooks, reactions, and roles that were learned during childhood years by seeing those same events through more objective and more spiritual eyes.

Sometimes a person who has helped others along similar paths can provide part of this insight and thus alleviate some of the time and effort. Then we can become happier, more secure, and more productive Christians more quickly than we would otherwise. Transformation truly is a *process*—a renew*ing* not a renewal—a road toward our being perfected, the end of which is not reached until we see Christ face-to-face in heaven.

10

Abusers and the Church

A survey was conducted among readers of the quarterly magazine *Christian Psychology for Today* (published by the Minirth-Meier Foundation), to see what subjects they were most interested in learning about. Also queried was which issues they had found most helpful. Past issues carried themes such as "Maturing Successfully," "Burnout," "Christian Sexuality," "The Balanced Life," "Overcoming Negative Emotions," and "Eating Disorders."

The eating disorders issue discussed *anorexia nervosa*—eating miniscule amounts because of an intense fear of becoming obese, a fear that does not diminish as extreme weight loss progresses; *bulimia*—habitual eating in binges followed by forced purging (vomiting, multiple use of laxatives, diet pills, and other diuretics), in order not to gain weight; and *overeating*. The first two are prevalent today among 15 to 25 percent of young women ages 15 to 30. They include both psychological and spiritual roots.

One pastor wrote that he liked all the issues, except the one on "Eating Disorders," which he said wasn't needed. He would probably be surprised to learn that, unless his is a very small church indeed, there is great likelihood that several or more of its members secretly suffer from one of these deadly eating disorders. To prove our point, that issue was the first for which more requests were received than copies were available. Many pastors are unaware of the burdens that their members carry behind a "happy Christian facade."

The Hidden Trauma

Another hidden and deadly disorder among numerous church members is drug and alcohol abuse. Many pastors think substance abuse cannot be a problem in their church, particularly if their church emphasizes abstinence. As we have shown, however, no church today can distance itself from such problems. Not only do many church members suffer with substance abuse, either directly or indirectly, but so do church leaders.

The problems stay secret for two reasons: (1) a misunderstanding of how the Holy Spirit helps believers; (2) a misunderstanding of the use of church discipline.

Choosing Drug Dependency Over "Others" Dependency

In some circles of Christianity, when experiencing stress it is more acceptable to use a drug than to ask for help from other people. Turning to drugs—even to drug dependency—is more accepted and creates less guilt than turning to other people—to believer dependency. Particularly is this so when the drugs considered are legal ones and include aspirin; prescription drugs; and alcohol-laced, over-the-counter cure-alls, as well as ordinary alcohol drinks.

The mind-frame of depending on God, not man, that many Christians practice fails to take into consideration the fact that God often works through other people on their behalf.

Some Christians think that believers are not supposed to depend on other people but only on the Holy Spirit within them. Not understood is the concept that we also need to depend on the Holy Spirit as it is *manifested through other Christians.* "Now to each one the manifestation of the Spirit is given for the common good" (1 Cor. 12:7).

At the same time, we acknowledge the tendency for many addicts, who already have or who develop passive-dependent personalities, to lean on others too much to do everything for them. Then when disappointed, they may stop asking and start blaming others for all their problems, with the notion that they won't receive *any* help (or at least the all-inclusive help they want), even if they do ask.

Between these two extremes lies the truth about the help of the Holy Spirit. It is important to realize that God is a god of order. He balances his use of the Holy Spirit within a person with his use of the manifestation of the Spirit through other people. The Holy Spirit, through others, more often offers advice, guidance, love, and encouragement regarding how one can help and do things for oneself, with just enough physical help to take away the *over*burden. This leaves a person with a major but manageable part of the responsibility for his or her own life.

Pastoral Drug Abuse

The path of looking to aspirins, then prescription drugs, then alcohol, in order to relieve emotional pain, rather than the path of admitting a need for help from others, is a temptation to which pastors and other church leaders are especially vulnerable. They are more likely than other Christians not to seek the help of the Holy Spirit as manifested through other believers. After all, they are supposed to be models of Christian strength, people who need only God. They are expected to solve all the problems of other Christians without having problems themselves.

Because of this imposed need to appear nearer perfect than the average church member, the special pressures experienced by ministering couples, and the need to seek an alternative relief from burdens, substance abuse among church leaders may emerge as much if not more than within the population in general.

An added problem in some churches that use real wine for communion involves a situation that has often been joked about—the tendency of clerics to finish off leftover communion wine themselves and getting tipsy. The reality is no joke however. Numbers of clergymen who have been treated for alcoholism have become addicted in just this way.

As astounding as it may seem, it is not an overstatement to say that as many as 10 percent of ministers and ministers' wives may be drug abusers. Like Sally, the pastor's wife who became addicted to Valium, it isn't likely that they will abuse illegal drugs, but overall they are just as likely to abuse the use of other drugs. Since the ratio of pastors and pastors' wives with psychological or physical tendencies toward alcoholism will be the same as within the population in general, clergy alcoholism is not at all unusual.

Case Example: Chuck, the Evangelist

A typical pattern, which has been known to create alcoholism in a number of ministers of the gospel, is vividly illustrated in the case of Chuck, an evangelist we treated. Chuck grew up with a lot of obsessive traits and some hysterical and dependency (passive-aggressive) traits.

He was an only child and only children tend to develop the worst of all three of the above personality traits. They have parents who expect their one little darling to be perfect. If this only child also has a domineering, unaffectionate mother and a passive father, as Chuck had, he is likely to develop hysterical personality traits too, craving maternal affection and attention.

Chuck carried this over to craving the attention of other females (whom he unknowingly equated with his mother). To receive their attention, he became quite a performer, as most hysterical personalities do. He acted in plays and sang and played musical instruments in high school.

Although his mother did not pay much attention to Chuck as a person, she did tend to bail him out of situations in which he acted irresponsibly. This created sociopathic traits in him, in which he felt he could get away with "murder" and that the world owed him a living. He usually thought it was the fault of other people when he got in trouble, since his mother never made him accept the consequences of his irresponsible actions.

When Chuck dedicated his life to Christ, his hysterical tendencies gave him a strong desire, like that of many Christian hysterics, to be an evangelist—a person who sways an audience, for a worthwhile cause, of course—and to feel called to being such.

Separating Call from Desire

Of course, many hysterical (histrionic) personalities really are called to be evangelists. Perhaps one reason God calls them to a platform ministry is partly because they do feel happier and more secure in front of an audience, and because they have learned from early days how to interest, communicate, and hold an audience's attention. But when a person has a seemingly natural, emotional desire to interact with an audience anyway, it is reason to examine the urge for a platform ministry very carefully. The hysteric personality needs to determine whether this desire is primarily an attempt to meet personal emotional needs, masked by the normal Christian desire to communicate the good news of Christ, or is truly a call from God for this particular type of ministry. If it involves both, the histrionic evangelist must constantly review, preferably with objective help from someone else—wife, close friend or associate, or personal pastor—which drive is motivating him.

Seeing Our Own Sin Clearly

Chuck also had a lot of dependency traits. He felt others were to blame or were responsible for both his good and bad emotions, actions, and habit patterns. This he denied to himself, however. Because of this denial, he strongly resented drug and alcohol addicts, and whenever he was around any he felt nauseated by them. The reason was that they reminded him of traits inside himself that he was not acknowledging and facing up to. Chuck's situation is one of those described by the apostle Matthew in Matthew 7:1–5.

> "Do not judge, or you too will be judged. For in the same way you judge others, you will be judged, and with the measure you use, it will be measured to you.
> Why do you look at the speck of sawdust in your brother's eye and pay no attention to the plank in your own eye? How can you say to your brother, 'Let me take the speck out of your eye,' when all the time there is a plank in your own eye? You hypocrite, first take the plank out of your own eye, and then you will see clearly to remove the speck from your brother's eye."

In his evangelistic crusades, Chuck primarily preached against alcohol and drugs, since he hated addicts. They reminded him of himself so much, although he didn't know this was why he hated this particular sin so intensely.

The life of an evangelist, of course, is not a settled one. Traveling a lot, experiencing lonely motel rooms, and lacking the security of home and family, this alcohol hater eventually began drinking himself—and to excess.

In psychiatry a strong dislike for a particular sin or weakness because of one's own tendencies toward it is called a *reaction formation*. Chuck's reaction formation would have been evident to many who are psychologically trained, even before he began drinking.

Of course, to diagnose Chuck's own tendencies toward substance abuse, particularly before Chuck began drinking, would have been only to incur anathema for most Christians, who, at least until the 1987-88 highly publicized media evangelists' frays, tended to hold clergy as above all that. Of course we all need to be aware that "there but for the grace of God go I." However, to know, deep down, that a certain weakness applies in a particular way to you or, even more, to someone (clergyman, political figure, or other) whom you hold in high esteem, is very hard for many people to accept.

Once Chuck began drinking, it didn't take long before his psychological traits helped him become alcoholic. As with all alcoholics, the inhibitory centers of Chuck's brain were numbed, so eventually Chuck started having sexual affairs during his traveling crusades. The unmet need for childhood maternal attention, of course, made him more vulnerable to this particular type of sin.

Chuck's Christian conscience attacked these actions, producing a strong sense of guilt. To counteract the guilt, Chuck justified his behavior by telling himself that he had affairs only with women who wanted them, women whom he met in bars, not Christian, church-going women. Blaming the women rather than himself was a type of thinking that was easier for him than for many others, since from childhood on he had never had to face up to his own faults.

When Chuck came to us with his alcohol problem, we did more than dry him out and treat the physical disease of his alcoholism. And we did more than confront him with the "error of his ways." Through insight-oriented therapy, we revealed to him his personality tendencies and *why* he had adopted his particular justifications for his actions.

At first Chuck was very resistant to insight-oriented therapy. It was extremely painful for him to look at the truth of his personality. However, slowly he did gain insights into himself and began to grow and change, strengthening those weak areas of his personality. And eventually he did return to evangelism as a responsible evangelist. His outlook on those who sin, and particularly on those whose sins involve substance abuse, is far different today than it was before.

Richard Meier, a former pastor now on our counseling staff,

also admits to previously trying to rebuke substance abusers out of their sin and administer a "quick fix," instead of helping them out of their sin. Now both Richard and Chuck emphasize *how to deal* with what is wrong in an alcoholic's and addict's life, instead of emphasizing *what* is wrong in their lives.

Exhorting Versus Encouraging

Often passive-dependent, addictive personalities, when rebuked to "straighten up and fly right," or even to "shape up or ship out" (which is also not a biblical exhortation), don't know how. They have never learned *how* to use their willpower. They have never learned what depending on God truly means, which is to call on his Holy Spirit to help them *activate* their God-given willpower or self-control.

For instance, we have counseled scores of alcoholics who have said that they were still alcoholics because God had not taken their habit away from them. They actually blamed God for their continued addiction! They misquoted Isaiah 40:31 by saying they decided to "wait upon the LORD" (KJV). They often latched on to Christian lingo such as "Let go and let God." Then they *let go* of whatever puny grasp they had of their self-control and *waited* for God to make their addictions go away. The only problem was that their addictions never went away. God doesn't work that way. Philippians 4:13 says, "I can do all things *through Christ,* who *strengthens me*" (italics added).

(As a matter of clarification, the phrase "Let go and let God" may be good advice for the obsessive-compulsive, self-driven person who has depended too much on self, but not for the passive-dependent or some other personalities.)

Isaiah the prophet told us that those who *wait* upon the Lord will have renewed strength, will soar like eagles, will run and not grow weary, and will walk and not faint (Isa. 40:29–31). This is probably one of the most misused verses in the Bible. According to a Hebrew professor at Dallas Theological Seminary, "Wait on the Lord" means that we *rely* or *depend on* God for spiritual strength; he will exchange his strength for our weakness so that *we can exert* our God-assisted *self-control* to do what God wants us to do. God will not wave a magic wand when we just sit and wait for him to make all our addictions (or other problems) go away.

Addicts, however, need some help in learning these things, rather than just being exhorted to do them.

Looking for Signs

Many church members conceal alcoholism for years. They will go to their pastor for family problems and personal difficulties, without ever revealing their root cause of substance abuse. Often, they are unwilling to admit to themselves that this has anything to do with it. If anything, they believe that the substance abuse is only a way to *escape* their problems; they do not admit that it is a major cause of the problems. Even after people with strong credentials in addiction diagnosis and therapy face the church members with their addiction, they are still unwilling to believe the extent of their problem or that they can't conquer it on their own. As their addiction progresses, they eventually drop out of church altogether, often believing they have lost their salvation.

Pastors and other church counselors need to be sensitive toward the possibility of this more pervasive, unrevealed cause of the many problems some church members and their families encounter. This is where the Christian therapist or psychologist often has an edge in helping Christians who harbor secret sins. However, a pastor can become more aware of and learn how to handle many such underlying problems too, through books and seminars held in their area on Christian counseling and on addictive substances.

The Pastor's Attitude

A pastor's attitude toward substance abuse will also set the tone for how the rest of the church will minister to addicts or their families. A church is more likely to be a ministering church to abusers and their families if the pastor agrees in principle and in practice to the following biblical and realistic fundamentals:

  to love the sinner while hating the sin

  to keep from grading certain sins as worse than others

  to realize that a walk down the aisle to repent of sinful behavior will not cure most addicts (although the unusual few have been cured this way. The founder of AA received an instant healing, but when he started encouraging other alcoholics, he found this didn't happen for them, so he developed the twelve-step system of AA.)

  to realize that substance abuse is both a sin and a disease

  to stress the need to get both addicts and their family members loving and knowledgeable Christian support (trained counselors and small, intimate sharing groups)

  to emphasize the fact that everyone is a pilgrim in the Christian life, working toward the practical realization of their completeness in Christ.

These can make all the difference in redeeming, in this world, the lives of the abuser and his family members. The church must offer hope, compassion, and acceptance to abusers.

Several pastors we know admit that the church has sometimes been harmful to abusers and their families. They have all seen numbers of people come forward in services to repent and turn against sins of substance abuse only to fall right back into their same problem. One pastor finally acknowledged that sometimes when pastors "take a strong stand against sin," they only wind up standing on the sinners' toes, wounding them yet further and killing further still any hope that they can change.

Disciplining the Substance Abuser

The church's role with the substance abuser is to get him or her to acknowledge the problem, to desire to change, and to seek help. Because addicts do not think clearly, the church needs to be ready to provide suggestions, make arrangements, and even provide transportation for the addict to receive treatment. If the addict at first agrees and then refuses to change or to go for help, then the church needs to keep working with the person. The church should offer help, a number of times, before they consider administering church discipline.

Discipline should be administered only when the abuser has again and again *refused even to acknowledge the problem* or to show any desire to change. If the abuser has shown a desire to change (repent), has made some attempt, but then has slipped back into his or her habit, the church's role is to provide even more help, not less, by expelling the addict from any possibility of contact from other believers.

The goal of church discipline is always:

To lead sinners to repentance.

Jesus said to his disciples: "Things that cause people to sin are bound to come. . . . If your brother sins, rebuke him, and if he repents, forgive him. If he sins against you seven times in a day, and seven times comes back to you and says, 'I repent,' forgive him." [It seems God knows the pull of human nature toward habitual sinning, even when the sinner wants to change.]

Luke 17:1, 3

To restore weaker brothers.

Brothers, if someone is caught in a sin, you who are spiritual should restore him gently. But watch yourself, or you also may be tempted. Carry each other's burdens. . . .

Gal. 6:1

To gradually *increase the severity of discipline,* depending
on how much the addict will listen to you, not according to how
many times he or she slips and falls again (as we have seen in
Luke 17 above).

> [Jesus said] "If your brother sins against you, go and show him
> his fault, just between the two of you. If he listens to you, you
> have won your brother over. But if he will not listen, take one or
> two others along, so that 'every matter may be established by
> the testimony of two or three witnesses.' If he refuses to listen
> to them, tell it to the church; and if he refuses to listen even to
> the church, treat him as you would a pagan. . . ."
>
> Matt. 18:15–17

To disassociate with continually *sinning,* unrepentant
*brothers, who make no attempts, even unsuccessful ones, to
change.*

> . . . you must not associate with anyone who calls himself a
> brother but [continually] is sexually immoral or greedy, an idol-
> ater or a slanderer, a drunkard or a swindler. With such a man
> do not even eat. . . . Expel the wicked man from among you.
>
> 1 Cor. 5:11, 13b

To forgive and restore the repentant (who had been expelled
because of prior unrepentance) *to fellowship.*

> The punishment inflicted on him by the majority is sufficient
> for him. Now instead, you ought to forgive and comfort him, so
> that he will not be overwhelmed by excessive sorrow. I urge
> you, therefore, to reaffirm your love for him.
>
> 2 Cor. 2:6–8

Providing Support for the Family

Often the substance abuser already is or has become an inactive church member. The abuser's family may be more ac-

tive, using the church as a haven from a chaotic family life. The church must be sure that whatever discipline is given to the abuser does not drive the family away from church as well.

Once the whole church knows of the church's discipline of the abuser, other church members may shy away from associating not just with the abuser but with his or her family as well, when just the opposite reaction should occur. And even if church members do not back away from the family, the family is likely to shy away from fellow Christians out of embarrassment and shame, now that their "awful family secret" is in the open. The abuser's family needs special love and support from other Christians on a frequent basis now, and not just on Sunday mornings.

Providing Assistance for the Abuser

Christian love and support for the abuser's family will also act as a promise to the expelled addict that the same is available to him or her once repentance is made and the road toward recovery is begun.

A church in Montgomery, Alabama, collected money for the treatment of an alcoholic member, mailed him get-well cards while he was at the treatment facility, prayed for him daily, and, upon his return from treatment, welcomed him home— like the prodigal son was welcomed home—with a tremendous celebration.

Institutional Referrals

The church needs to know the availability of facilities in their area that will treat substance abusers physically, psychologically, and spiritually. At the same time, it should not take whatever referrals it receives about such institutions for granted. The pastor or an elder should interview someone in authority regarding referring church members to that facility before any need to do so comes up. Questions asked should include the emphasis on all three areas of needed treatment: the physical, psychological, and spiritual. If the facility's staff does not provide Christian spiritual therapy, ask if they allow *and cooperate with* outside Christian therapists, as "fellow professionals," to visit the patient on the premises.

Support Groups

When the shrill ring of the bedside telephone awoke a pastor from a sound sleep a few years ago, he found an anguished church member on the other end, pouring out a story of another failure in his long-term battle to stay away from alcohol. This Christian had tried many alcohol cures, all of which helped for a while, but then he would slip again.

After praying with him on the telephone, the pastor told him to get some sleep, but made the man promise to see him the next day, no matter what.

This distraught man, who tried hard to stay sober, was then introduced to a recently formed support group, the members of which were all helping one another overcome severely ingrained habits. That was many years ago, and this Christian hasn't had another drink since. Meanwhile he has gone on to help many other members of his church keep free from whatever habits were enslaving them.

When recovering addicts are released from institutional care, they need a group of people who will help them keep on the straight and narrow. Without that, they may do fine for a while, but when trauma or other temptations again lure them to look for escape in substance abuse, they may find their growing but still shaky willpower or new ways of thinking need a boost from other people and their insights. Left on their own, they are one day likely to succumb. With the help of other people available at the moment of temptation, they may ride out the crisis.

The church needs to see the addict not as a burden to them and a slave to his habit, which he currently is, but through time, therapy, and supportive encouragement as a potential servant of God.

The Church Plus AA

For those Christians whose churches do not have a similar program, we recommend Alcoholics Anonymous as part of their therapy but not for their total recovery. They need insight-oriented therapy and an emphasis on biblical hope for total recovery, but AA does help them keep in control, gives them a more realistic perspective, and gives them someone to share their struggles with, other than their counselor.

Alcoholics Anonymous has benefited thousands of people. They do get people to face up to the fact that alcoholism is a personal problem that each alcoholic individual needs to accept, own up to, and take responsibility for. We like that aspect of it.

Having regular meetings is a good strength of AA for people to verbalize their feelings and to look at the truth and share it with each other, realizing that they are not the only ones in the world with the problem. Almost any programs that work in the area of alcohol and drug abuse are programs that do involve working with the support of other people. In that sense AA helps to drum up some of that support.

Alcoholics Anonymous has to avoid getting very theological, because there are people of all religious backgrounds who go to AA. It is a public group. Thus they address God, depending on which chapter meetings you go to, as "some being out there somewhere." Some groups are more Christian than others. Some groups do talk about God as who he is and that Christ is God. Generally, however, the weakness of AA from a Christian perspective is that it is not a specifically biblically oriented program. However, to be a public group, they need to be what they are. They do a good job to help a lot of people.

The *church* ought to be an important resource through which the Christian addict or the addict's family can seek help. These same principles of Alcoholics Anonymous can be used to better advantage when zeroed in on the centrality of Christ. Only within the church or interchurch Christian groups is that likely to happen. Some Christian addicts have been versed enough in their theology to reapply AA's general references to a "higher power" to their previous Christian training and have found their way back to Christ through AA. Other less knowledgeable or less believing Christians have overcome their drinking habits in AA but, in the process, have become doubtful of the importance of Christianity, since it was not what helped them in their hour of need.

The Christian writer, Philip Yancey, tells of meeting a deeply committed Christian at an AA meeting who had "put his intellectual faith in abeyance while struggling with simple survival" (Yancey 1983). The AA "church" keeps him sober. The Christian church now seems irrelevant, vapid, and gutless to him. Others in AA groups tell stories of rejection, judgment, and "guilt trips" given them by Christians. In AA they are accepted as worthwhile people. If they go to church, they feel inferior and incomplete, because other church members look at them with an air of piety or superiority. Members of AA must consciously lean on God (or their idea of God) and on each other. They don't see church members consciously doing that. (Possibly AA members lean on each other too much, of course, since they are generally dependent-type personalities, and AA does not change that. However, Christians probably should lean on and reach out to each other more than many of them do, especially through overburdening trials.)

Al-Anon

Al-Anon, a subsidiary organization of Alcoholics Anonymous, fulfills a good function of providing support for families and friends of alcoholics. In many instances we encourage family members of alcoholics to become involved in Al-Anon. As mentioned previously, while Al-Anon's program refers to a nonspecific idea of God, it does include many important Christian principles, fellowship, support, and an opportunity to learn from and minister to fellow sufferers of families affected by chemical abuse.

The basic strengths and weaknesses of Al-Anon are the same as those of AA. Many pastors regularly use Al-Anon as a valuable resource tool for families of alcoholics. Usually it is more helpful for local churches to provide, from a biblical perspective, the primary means of support for families and friends of alcoholics.

Many churches or groups of like-minded small churches use recovered alcoholics and their families in group sessions and one-on-one to provide fellowship and help in practical, tangible ways to family members of substance abusers. The individuals in the program are the most important aspect of such groups. They need to be committed to the value of this endeavor as a ministry and be willing to put the time and effort it takes into the families of substance abusers.

Christian Support Groups

If there is a Christian counterpart to AA available, if some church has an AA-type program, then we recommend recovering alcoholics or families of alcoholics attend that program, primarily because it would be geared to their doctrine, their beliefs, and to the Bible.

In our years of pastoral and psychiatric counseling, one of the most effective tools we've found to overcome addictions is believers' meeting together, to help each other overcome harmful addictive habits—whether substance abuse, workaholism, TV viewing, eating disorders, or explosive anger. A pastor, therapist, or other trained leader to lead or attend the group is not really necessary. A proven method to use with the group is a Christian adaptation of the AA Twelve Steps.

To start such a group, with church members suffering from various addictive problems, you may want to refer to the Minirth-Meier Clinic booklet *Helping One Another Change Bad Habits* (Moody Press, 1987), which is a part of Moody's Acorn Series.

Other Christian organizations that deal only with alcoholics or drug abusers already may have groups meeting in your community. If not, their offices will tell you how to start such a group. Some of these are:

Alcoholics Victorious
International Office
C/o Chicago Christian Industrial League
123 South Green St.
Chicago, IL 60607
(312) 421-0588

Overcomers Outreach, Inc.
2290 W. Whittier Blvd., Suite D
La Habra, CA 90631
(213) 697-3994

Substance Abusers Victorious
One Cascade Plaza, Suite 1222
Akron, OH 44308
(216) 253-5444

11

Preventing Addiction in the Next Generation

In spite of genuine efforts to be thoroughly Christian, some Christian families still have patterns which can reinforce substance abuse.

Based on extensive work with drug abusers in the New York City area, Dennis Reilly (1979) compiled characteristics of families which tend to "push" a troubled youth into drug abuse. Each of these characteristics have also been observed in cases we have seen, even among practicing Christian families. Make sure your family atmosphere is made of the opposite of these.

Characteristics of Addict-producing Families

Negativism. Communication in the family occurs primarily in negative ways. There is criticism, blaming, nagging, and correcting (correcting grammar, manners, feelings,

149

disgusting habits)—always correcting. And then there is the silent treatment. The child in this environment eventually learns that by creating trouble he or she can get attention or get the parents talking to each other. On the other hand, the child also learns that acceptable behavior is ignored—it doesn't pay off.

Parental inconsistency. In many drug-abusing families, parents have difficulty setting clear rules and are inconsistent in enforcing them. To make it worse, one parent often counters and undermines the rules of the spouse.

Vicarious parental pleasure. Some parents have secret wishes to pursue pleasures for which they lusted as a child and felt deprived of enjoying. The forbidden sins of their youth are now being indulged secondhand by providing their children opportunities to "enjoy" irresponsible behavior in breaking school rules, disobeying traffic laws, and even in sex, violence, drugs, or general lifestyle. Then they pump their children for all the juicy details of their escapades in a stern third-degree questioning. Later on the parents can be heard repeating the stories with gleeful laughter. In this manner the parents are able to enjoy the indulgence while the children are left to experience the costly consequences.

Unexpressed anger. Related to negativism in families discussed above, families which have trouble expressing feelings in general are more vulnerable to drug and alcohol abuse. When in conflict, a member may shut off expression of love and acceptance. This can lead to a child's frustration, anger, deprivation, and rage. The rage cannot be expressed directly without some risk, so the youth in such a family uses indirect means to discharge his or her anger. Drug abuse is a passive-aggressive way of getting revenge. It is an act of rebellion. As Dennis Reilly (1979) points out, many young people will say, "If my parents knew I used drugs, it would kill them." Then they arrange to get caught in a way designed to be as embarrassing as possible to their parents.

Unrealistic parental expectations. Parents of drug-abusing children have often been unrealistic in their expectations. This is a common threat in homes of ministers or church leaders who are trying hard to have a model family. In some churches leaders are painfully aware that their children's behavior is critically being observed. By selectively praising performance that meets the highest standards and shutting off any affirmation of worth when performance falls anywhere below the high-water mark, the parent causes the young person to become discouraged or angry. Drugs or alcohol not only are used for revenge; they also are used as an excuse or escape from the parental demands. After all, parents can't expect too much from a kid who has a drug or alcohol problem, especially if they believe that addiction to a drug is a disease.

On the other end of the spectrum, some parents think their child will never amount to much. If the child had problems as an infant with temporary, delayed development in the first years of life, the parents may expect the worst and pay too much attention—even panic—at the normal problems in development. The child gets the message that he is inadequate and isn't expected to do well. He or she plays out these negative expectations to give the parents what they want and to match his own life-script.

Self-medication. Families who have a pattern of using mood-altering substances to reduce headaches, tension, or anxiety are good candidates for substance abuse. The message is passed on that all pain is unbearable. Rather than using pain as a motivator to find and correct the underlying cause of pain, the receptors in the body are deadened to avoid dealing with the issue.

The Making of an Addict

Using this same negative warning method and with tongue in cheek, we now tell parents how to make their preschool children into drug addicts or alcoholics. These rules are especially easy to fall into with a youngest child, because parents hate to see that youngest child grow up, ready to leave the nest, and no longer needing individual attention.

1. Spoil them; give them everything they want if you can afford it.
2. When they do wrong, you may nag them, but never spank them (unless they are showing signs of independence).
3. Foster their dependence on you, so drugs or alcohol can replace you when they are older.
4. Protect them from your spouse and from all those mean teachers who threaten to spank them from time to time. Sue them if you wish.
5. Make all their decisions for them, since you are a lot older and wiser than they are. They might make mistakes and learn from them if you don't.
6. Criticize their other parent openly, they, particularly as the other parent's same sex offspring, can lose their own self-respect and confidence.
7. Always bail them out of trouble so they will like you. Besides, they might harm your reputation if they get a police record. Never let them suffer the consequences of their own behavior.
8. Always step in and solve their problems for them, so they can depend on you and run to you when the going gets tough. Then when they are older and still haven't learned how to solve their own problems, they can continue to run from problems through drugs or alcohol.
9. Take lots of prescription drugs yourself, so that taking nonprescription drugs won't be a major step for them.

As stated earlier, drug addiction and alcoholism are a continuing choice, a choice usually made by people with dependent-personality disorders. They generally come from families where there was an absent, passive, or uninvolved father and an overcontrolling mother who spoiled them exces-

sively. Being the youngest or only boy in the family is a factor
which gives their mothers added temptations to spoil them.
Many times, they are the only alcoholic or drug addict in an
otherwise normal family, and they consider themselves the
black sheep of the family.

If Your Husband Is an Addict

The wife of an alcoholic needs *to try to build a husband and
dad image where there is none.* It is very easy to fall into the
trap of running Dad down. Do just the opposite. Help your
children see the positive aspects of their father and help them
see where he is struggling under a sin problem, just as we all
are. In a sense, that helps the child develop some sense of a
positive father image, even though Dad may not be much of a
model himself.

That father image is going to have a lot to do with the
child's later concept of God. If the only concept of God they get
from Dad is a drinking, irrational, sometimes loving, sometimes punishing, sometimes hugging, sometimes hitting,
kind of all-powerful being, then when they grow up, they are
going to have a hard time believing that you can count on God,
even after they become Christians. So even if Dad isn't worth
it, Mom can help the child develop a fairly positive image
toward him and the father role, which will help the child in his
or her walk with God. Unconditional love for a mate plays a
key role in the Christian life.

The second major approach is to *try to build a second family
around that child,* key people in the child's environment who
can provide some of the nurturance, stability, and positive
self-image input that the child needs. Loving and stable members of the extended family are one possibility. A good school
situation is helpful, as is a good community-athletic program,
where the child can develop self-esteem. The church is the
only institution that can truly meet all those needs however.
When the church gets working, it can provide fatherly contacts, peer-group support, and lots of nurturance—spiritually

and psychologically, and sometimes even physically—to offset a child's fears about the family at home.

Positive Addictions to Healthy Situations

For years researchers wondered why people experienced a "high" when they took drugs. In order for drugs to have such an effect, there had to be receptors in the brain to which they could attach. And if there were receptors in the brain to which opium and other types of drugs, introduced from outside the body, could attach, it would seem that they were designed to receive natural "uppers" manufactured within the body.

In recent years we have been able to identify these. They are called *endorphins*. These endorphins can be released and attached to their receptors in response to a positive stimuli. Thus one can actually develop a positive addiction to healthy situations. For example, many individuals, may probably develop a positive addiction to running and other sports. It is also very possible that one can develop a positive addiction to spiritual matters. One actually can be "high on Christ," rather than "high" on unhealthy and deadly substances. How long-lasting that high will be, however, will depend on one's relative physical and emotional health and activity. Some of the endorphins produced from positive activity in one area of a person's life can be destroyed by poor habits or sickness in another area.

This knowledge was the answer to questions Frank Minirth had had since college days, when he came into contact with Christians who seemed "high on Christ." This was at a time when college students getting high on drugs was a new and growing problem—when drug abuse was primarily a collegiate phenomenon.

Frank Minirth recalls those observations from college days.

"I've never seen anyone so excited about Christ. They actually seem 'high' as they share Bible verses and talk about the Lord. They certainly are different."

On and on the thoughts rambled through my head. I was in my first year of college. Drug abuse was at a zenith, but I was wrestling with a far different problem. I felt a spiritual longing. I longed to walk with the Lord and yet, I was not close to him, and I knew it.

Living on campus, I was not able to withstand all the problems I faced so I began to commute from home (about thirty miles). A young assistant minister from my local church asked to commute with me. I had already seen that this young minister was "high" on Christ. He would sing the old hymns of the faith and talk about Jesus. He knew Christ as no one I had ever met. He stressed only Christ and avoided any issues that might distract from him.

We had both heard about a Bible study on campus and decided to attend. The teacher enjoyed Bible verses like I enjoyed my favorite food. His eyes glistened as he talked about Christ. His voice would echo with excitement as he shared about the Lord. I was deeply impressed but I must admit, I was skeptical. Could a person just be "high" on Christ alone? Or was he faking his enthusiasm?

As the months went on, these Christians' testimonies remained true. I began to capture some of my Bible teacher's enthusiasm. I had a long way to go, but I could feel the beginning of that closeness with the Lord. I could feel the emotions soar as I memorized "Be anxious for nothing," "Peace I leave with you," "Casting all your care upon him, for he careth for you," "I will never leave thee, nor forsake thee." My old black Bible became worn.

Then life took another dramatic turn. I had been a rather lonely teenager, but now I had met a godly, young lady. She was absolutely beautiful. Again, I was struck with the fact that she too was "high" on Christ, but with a quiet and gentle spirit. I was surprised she would even consider marrying me but she did.

The years went on and I continued to fight back, but my roughest challenge—medical school—still lay ahead. I had always been at the top of my class, but for the first time I met my match. The courses were unbelievably hard. The students were unbelievably smart. I felt exhausted. I was becoming more and more discouraged.

Then God's sovereignty intervened once again. I discovered that a project mate in one class was also a Christian, but he wasn't just another Christian. He shared how he had given his life to the Lord to use in medicine. He wanted to have an effect for Christ. Several elderly, godly saints had been praying for him for years. He must not disappoint them, he said, and even more important, he must not disappoint Christ. He had a destiny he must find. He too was "high" on Christ.

We became close Christian friends. Together we sat down and asked ourselves how we could have an effect for Christ in our lifetime. That friend was Paul Meier.

Answers for the Christian Family

Drug abuse is preventable. To raise children who will not say yes to drugs, we would recommend the following seven steps.

Lead your child to Christ. We live in an unstable, stressful world. We need a powerful friend in order to face that world. Christ can be such a friend.

We should not assume our children know Christ just because they grew up in a Christian home. We also should not assume our children know Christ because they "walked the aisle of a church," "made a commitment to Christ," "were baptized," and so forth. Individuals have to make the choice of receiving Christ into their lives personally, trusting Christ to be their own Savior from the eternal consequences of their sin.

Then, as Christians, if Christ's power is to be available to them, they must realize it was not so much that they gave their lives to Christ; rather it was that they received Christ's life. They are not to give, but to receive; they are not to commit, but to accept. The commitment, the work, the life, all follow when Christ indwells that person. When they realize that they have received Christ's life, then they will realize that they are now able to do what, as hopeless sinners and imperfect human beings, they could never have done otherwise. They can now withstand temptations because of Christ's indwelling life.

Model a healthy life.   Children model after their parents. A child watching a parent smoke to relax, drink to relieve pressure, take tranquilizers, and so forth, will easily turn to drugs personally later in life. He or she is simply programmed that way.

A teen who sees a parent "high" on Christ will more likely become on fire for the Lord, too. We are impressed with the need to have God as a routine, daily part of life, to share freely Scripture verses at home, to sing old hymns of the faith, to pray for our children's needs with them daily. (Read again Deuteronomy 6:7.)

Spend time with your teen.   President Reagan appointed a commission on the family to study healthy families. One of the six qualities found that healthy families possess was spending time together. Many teens that come in our hospital wards admit that they abuse drugs to get their parents' attention. Some researchers say that no country has parents that spend less time with their children than those of the USA, except perhaps England. One study revealed that American fathers spend an average of thirty-seven seconds per day with their children! Although that study seemed to spur many on to try to correct that, later studies revealed only a few minutes a day were all the improvement that had been made. Psychiatric research has also confirmed that the greatest influence on a young person is not his peers but his family. This is true even in the adolescent years. They long to be with us, even if they don't always admit that. Give them that time.

Utilize peer groups.   Whereas the family is the most important factor in a teen's life, peers are nôt unimportant.

Christian peer groups can do several things: give good role
models outside the family; help direct the energy of adolescence; promote healthy competition; and help youths to deal
with their idealism and zest for life.

Get help for the whole family.   If one family member
has problems, it is only an indication of problems in the entire
family. The whole family system will need help, not just an individual part of that system. Family counseling can often be
of much help through improving conflict resolution, communication, and commitment to each other (three other qualities
consistently found in healthy families by President Reagan's
commission).

Attend church regularly.   Church is one of only two institutions (family is the other) set up by God. The local church
may not be perfect, but it is God's institution and he will bless
it. It offers support and the strength needed to stand against
the world. If your church does not have a strong and spiritual
youth program, find one that does, or at least introduce and
encourage your youth to become involved in an interchurch or
interdenominational youth program.

Dare your child to be a Daniel.   Daniel was a Bible
character who dared to stand alone because he had conviction.
He stood alone knowing it could cost him his life. He continued to pray to God after an order not to do so, punishable by
death, had been declared. The story from that point is a famil-
iar one. He withstood the lions' den because God was with
him. There is an old hymn that goes:

> Dare to be a Daniel.
> Dare to stand alone.
> Dare to have a purpose firm.
> Dare to make it known.

Teenagers and even preteens need to be challenged to stand
apart from peers when necessary—but not alone—for they will

be standing with Christ, in his strength and love. To do this they will have to spend time in God's Word in order to be strong and close to Christ. The apostle John stated:

> I write to you, young men,
> because you are strong,
> and the word of God lives in you,
> and you have overcome the evil
>   one."
>
> 1 John 2:14b

Although we personally never felt inclined to turn to drugs to escape problems, there were a number of times that we needed to experience a "high" to escape physical, mental, and spiritual stresses and struggles. We all wrestle with insecurities inside and may fall prey to many pitfalls. For many, the pitfall is drugs or alcohol, which reaches out with the promise of a good feeling but later turns into a downward cycle of destruction—of the mind, the body, and the spirit.

By God's grace, we may choose to avoid the pitfall of drugs or alcohol and rather be "high" on Christ. Our prayer is that churches, Christians, and their families may all be on that kind of "high."

Appendix: Personality Disorders Involved in Addictions

The Passive-Aggressive Personality

According to our findings in treating thousands of alcoholic and drug addicts, more than half have strong passive-dependent (passive-aggressive) personality traits.

Behavior Patterns

In this personality disorder both passivity and aggressiveness are evident. As expressed in *Introduction to Psychology and Counseling* (Meier 1982):

> Individuals with the disorder are inwardly aggressive but express their aggressive tendencies passively. They express anger, for example, primarily in subtle, nonverbal ways, rarely openly and verbally. The behavior of passive-aggressive individuals is an expression of resentment at failure to receive gratification from an individual or institution on which they are overly dependent. Resentful at not having their emotional needs met by others, they become very passive in their response to others, learning to accomplish their goals by passive manipulation. They look to others to give them direction and to take responsibility. Helpless and unwilling to be alone or to make a decision, they are the classic clinging vine. Their

main symptoms surface in their relationship to authority, society's demands, or the needs of others in a close personal relationship.

Behavior patterns characteristic of passive-aggressive or passive-dependent individuals include:

Obstructionism.   A passive-aggressive woman, for example, if angry with her husband over an incident that happened on Saturday night, may be obstructive on Sunday morning by being late in getting ready for church, especially if her husband is compulsive about being on time for church. Without doing so consciously, she may be unable to find her lipstick or shoes, causing a delay, and thus passively expressing her aggression toward him.

Pouting.   After a disagreement, a passive-aggressive person, instead of resolving it maturely, will pout and walk away.

Procrastination.   A passive-aggressive son, when asked by his mother to mow the yard, may express his hostility by putting it off.

Intentional inefficiency.   When the son can no longer get by through procrastination, he may exhibit intentional inefficiency, another method of passively expressing aggression. He may mow the yard but intentionally leave streaks and do a poor job. If as a result of that inefficiency he is relieved of the task, he has learned how to avoid responsibility.

Passive-aggressive personalities reach goals indirectly, learning to manipulate people by their passive behavior. Many of them, spoiled as children, expect the world to wait on them hand and foot the way their parents did.

Causes

Passive-aggressive personality develops when a person's dependency needs exceed normal limits. Some parents overprotect their children and have mixed reactions to them. This encourages a helpless, clinging attitude and inhibits development of independence as a result of their own guilt feelings.

Expecting other people to gratify all their needs, the children grow up dependent on others to protect them or aid them in the performance of daily chores. They tend to have a low tolerance for frustration. Basically insecure, they seek constant reminders of being loved. With their unfulfilled needs producing anger and depression, they feel very alone. Craving for satisfaction may lead to excessive eating, drinking, smoking, or use of addictive substances. A majority of cases of both drug addiction and alcoholism stem from a passive-aggressive personality disorder.

Because they need so much nurturance, passive-aggressives seek to please those on whom they depend and cannot tolerate criticism. The threat of any loss brings on anxiety. Unable to handle interpersonal tension, such individuals seek an infantile and blissful state.

The passive-aggressive personality, often produced by a domineering and controlling mother (or father), never learns to make independent decisions. Such individuals suffer anxiety when separated from their parent, sometimes developing a phobia to school and putting up a fuss to stay home. In school a boy like that may be the "teacher's pet" but his peers label him a "sissy" or a "momma's boy." Adult praise reinforces his passivity.

When he grows up he may perform well when told what to do, but have difficulty making his own decisions. A passive-aggressive male may choose a forceful mate or mother-substitute. Such a wife will probably soon tire of his dependency and seek divorce or lose herself in her children or a career. Feeling unloved and overburdened, the husband often seeks solace in alcohol, an outward gratification of his oral dependent needs. (A passive-aggressive woman generally has not faced the same kinds of conflicts, because male-dominated society has reinforced dependent behavior in women and encouraged them to be submissive.)

The passive-aggressive personality is sometimes developed as an expression of resentment against excessive parental demands. Such parents never meet the basic trust and dependency needs of their children. If open expression of hostility is not accepted by the parents, the children usually develop more subtle means of rebellious behavior. At the same time that the children are forced to repress resentment, their parents reject their affections and are basically hostile toward them. A cycle of inhibition and rejection develops. Such children soon learn that negative behavior (nail biting, bedwetting, eating problems) will at least get them attention, so they willingly take punishment at the price of greater gain.

Passive-aggressive children usually cause problems in school, violating class rules and frequently fighting with other students. By their teenage years they may lean toward the antisocial personality, engaging in delinquency, drug usage, and theft or other misdemeanors. If their passive aggression is better controlled and channeled constructively, such students may achieve academically but will never be popular socially because of their poor manner of relating to others. Passive-aggressives often use hypochondriacal complaints to escape duties imposed on them. Backaches, cramps, or migraine headaches can serve as a means of escaping from work.

In marital relationships, the passive-aggressive male is primarily concerned with his own gratification and may be unwilling to give much to his mate. Husbands who push their wives beyond their level of endurance cause many divorces. Their lack of adaptive skills and irritating personal habits make it difficult to establish satisfying personal relationships. Realizing that his dreams cannot be achieved as a result of his inadequacies may produce such bitterness and loss of self-esteem in a passive-aggressive male that he may contemplate suicide.

The Sociopath

As mentioned before, the sociopath is the user, the manipulator. Sociopathy is part of the teenage conflict, particularly between ages twelve through sixteen, where personalities are changing from seeing the world as something that revolves around them to a larger, "citizen-of-the world" concept of life. However, what appears to be sociopathy in a teenager may really be a result of depression or peer influence. If the child has always been manipulative, though, it may be true, ingrained sociopathy.

Sociopaths have repeated conflicts with society, with parents, with school, or with the law. However, if they are wealthy, they probably have no known history of such, since their parents have been able to buy off authorities to keep their kids' records clean and out of "serious trouble."

Those of us who are committed Christians need to avoid being used by sociopaths. But we need to balance this avoidance with Scripture. If someone wants to walk with us a mile, walk with him two. We need also to be gracious, to bear their overburdens, but also to let them bear their own rightful responsibilities and burdens. Both Psalm 118:8 and 146:30 say not to put your trust in man. It is not our responsibility to bail everybody out of their problems, particularly financial.

Sociopaths blame someone else for all their faults. If they steal a car, they'll blame the owner who left the keys in the car. They live by the pleasure principle, "If it feels good, do it."

The sociopath is (1) impulsive; (2) has a history of repeated trouble with people; (3) exhibits overt behavior that has spelled trouble for him or her in the past, particularly sexually.

He will say, "I love you," when he really means, "I like the way you make me feel," even if his actions hurt the other person or third parties. Sociopaths have even been known to pray before committing adultery.

Take warning not to get involved romantically with a sociopath, even if he says he is reformed. Young women who have a sociopathic father are in particularly grave danger of getting involved with sociopathic men. They will always "fall for" (have crushes on) sociopathic men. Other men will seem boring to them. Before marriage, sociopaths will seem very loving.

It is very hard, even for an experienced person, to spot socio-paths without knowing and analyzing all their behavior, in-cluding conduct they try to hide.

The Obsessive-Compulsive Personality

Clinically speaking, an obsession is a particular thought repeated over and over that is hard to dislodge from the mind. Such obsessions usually result in frequently repeated behav-ior patterns, which are known as compulsions.

Relatively normal obsessive-compulsive behavior, not nec-essarily in the disorder stage, would include a man who fre-quently pats his hip pocket to check to see if his wallet is still there; a housewife who calls her husband's office three times to remind him to come home early to visit with his in-laws; the Sunday school teacher who checks and cross-checks every Scripture reference to be used in his next lesson.

Extreme disorders that develop from the obsessive-compulsive personality include agoraphobia (fear of open places), panic attacks, anxiety attacks, an inability to sleep, and difficulty in functioning. These can lead to the need for hospitalization or intensive insight-oriented counseling to discover the root cause of the obsessions and their resulting components.

The obsessive-compulsive alcoholic will drink habitually, usually at the same time every day, ingesting the same bever-age.

The obsessive-compulsive personality (Minirth, et al 1978):

1. Is perfectionistic, neat, clean, orderly, dutiful, conscientious, meticulous, and moral.
2. Does a good job, but works too hard and is unable to relax.
3. Is choleric, overly conscientious, overly concerned, in-flexible, has an overly strict conscience and rigid thinking.

4. Rationalizes to deceive and defend self and intellectualizes in order to avoid emotions.

5. Is a good student, well organized, and interested in facts and not feelings; seems cold and stable, and tends to split hairs.

6. Is anti-authority at times and is pulled between actions of obedience and defiance. Obedience usually wins, but occasionally defiance wins. The obedience leads to rage, and the defiance leads to fear. The fears lead to perfectionistic traits, and the rage leads to non-perfectionistic traits. A basic problem is defiant anger.

7. Displays many opposite traits: conscientiousness and negligence, orderliness and untidiness.

8. Has three central concerns: dirt (he or she is very clean); time (he or she is punctual); and money (he or she wants a feeling of security).

9. Has feelings of helplessness, needs to be in control of self and others who are close to him or her, needs power, and is intensely competitive.

10. Keeps emotions a secret from others, feels with the mind (is too logical), and as a defense isolates feelings from whatever he or she is experiencing.

11. Has other defenses, including: *magical thinking* (thinking he or she has more power than what reality dictates); *reaction formation* (adopts attitudes and behavior that are opposite to the impulses the individual consciously or unconsciously harbors); and *undoing* (unconsciously acts out in reverse some unacceptable action that occurred in the past).

12. Struggles to bring conversations around to the level of theories.

13. Is afraid of feelings of warmth (which occurred in dependent relationships in early life); expresses anger more easily (because it encourages distance); postpones pleasure (out of unconscious guilt); lives in the future; lacks spontaneity; and is very insecure.

14. May have unspontaneous and routine sex with little

variety. Female perfectionists have difficulty with orgasm, and male perfectionists sometimes have difficulty with premature ejaculation. This is a result of anxiety, which is related to their fear of loss of control.

15. Usually had a parent or parents who were obsessive and demanded total devotion but gave minimal love, and who made the person feel accepted on a conditional basis (only when doing what the parent wanted him or her to do).

16. Often leans, intellectually and theologically, toward an extreme Calvinistic position, in which God chooses who will be saved and the individual's own actions, even the action of freely choosing to be saved, means little or nothing. (This is because he or she has a longing for some control in his or her uncertain world, as well as a desire to avoid personal responsibility.) Emotionally, however, he or she practices a distorted Arminian theological view, feeling he or she isn't good enough in his or her actions or personhood to warrant God's *continuing* salvation.

17. Needs respect and security.

18. Craves dependent relationships but fears them at the same time.

19. Needs to feel omnipotent and substitutes feelings of omnipotence for true coping.

20. Has trouble with commitment, fears loss of control, and frequently focuses on irrelevant details.

21. Often uses techniques to conceal anger, such as shaking hands frequently, with a handshake that is rigid.

22. Has feelings of powerlessness and avoids recognition of personal fallibility. He or she fears the possibility of being proven wrong, so lives in much doubt about personal words and actions. Even door latches are checked and rechecked to achieve certainty and security.

23. Is extraordinarily self-willed, uses his or her defense mechanisms to control aggressive impulses, and avoids real conflicts by dwelling on substitute obses-

sive thoughts. If these defense mechanisms do not work, the result is depression.

24. Is stubborn, stingy (with love and time), frugal, persistent, dependable in many ways, and reliable.

25. Has an overdeveloped superego, feels comfortable only when knowing everything, and tends to insist on ultimate truth in all matters.

26. Has exaggerated expectations of self and others.

27. Appears strong, decisive, and affirmative, but is not; rather he or she is uncertain, uneasy, and wavering. He follows rigid rules to control his uncertainty. He needs to *appear* perfect.

28. Exaggerates the power of personal thoughts. Words (spoken or unspoken) become a substitute for responsible action.

29. Has a grandiose self-view and strives to accomplish superhuman achievements to overcome insecurities. To this person, accepting one's limitations amounts to being average—and contemptible.

30. Is cautious in love relationships, because love results in concern about another's feelings that are not under one's own control.

31. Has a single-minded style of thinking; is good at tasks that require intense concentration; and believes that everything is either black or white—completely right or completely wrong.

32. Has a tendency to respond to extremes.

33. Is critical, but cannot stand criticism.

34. Has strong rituals in his or her personal religious system. Rituals are considered important in many other areas of life.

35. Considers commitment tantamount to dependency and being out of control. Marriage commitment is difficult; coexistence is preferred.

36. Lives in the future; saves for a tomorrow that never arrives, discounts limitations of time; and denies death.

37. Insists on honesty in marriage, which results in telling all at times.
38. Has trouble admitting mistakes.
39. Uses excessive cautions or restraints in courtship.
40. Gives minimal commitment in relationships, but demands maximal commitment. As a result, each marriage partner pursues his own interests and intimacy is limited. He or she is careful to do only a minimal share in marriage, but wants to think for both self *and* spouse.
41. Is legalistic in dealing with himself and others.
42. Is (a) pecuniary (obsessed with money matters); (b) parsimonious (very frugal or stingy); (c) pedantic (overly concerned with book knowledge and formal rules).

References Cited

Alcoholics Anonymous. (1955). New York: Alcoholics Anonymous Publishing Co., 5.

The American Psychiatric Association. (1980). *Quick Reference to the Diagnostic Criteria from DSM III,* 91–101.

Baekeland, F.; Lundwall, L.; and Kissin B. (1975). Methods of Treatment of Chronic Alcoholism: A Critical Appraisal. In R. J. Gibbins, Y. Israel, H. Kalant, R. Popham, W. Schmidt and R. G. Smart (Eds.), *Research Advances in Alcohol and Drug Problems* vol. 2. New York: John Wiley & Sons.

Bell, Verle, and Hawkins, Don. (1987). *Helping One Another Change Bad Habits.* Chicago Ill.: Moody Press.

Coleman, J. C. (1976). *Abnormal Psychology and Modern Life.* Glenview, Ill.: Scott Foresman and Co., 427.

Costello, R. M. (1975). Alcoholism Treatment and Evaluation, I, In Search of Methods. *International Journal of the Addictions* 10: 251–75.

Costello, R. M. (1975). Alcoholism Treatment and Evaluation, II, Collection of Two-Year Follow-Up Studies. *International Journal of the Addictions* 10: 857–68.

Currents in Affective Illness. (April 1987). Edited by Jack E. Rosenblatt and Nancy C. Rosenblatt, vol. 6, no. 4. Bethesda, Md.

"Did You Know That?" (1984). (Supplement #79 for Pastoral Counseling Course at Dallas Theological Seminary.)

Dobson, James. (1983). *Love Must Be Tough*. Waco, Tex.: Word Inc.

Dougherty, Ronald J., and Rush, Benjamin. (December 20, 1982). Drug Abuse. *Audio-Digest Family Practice,* vol. 30, no. 48.

Dunn, Jerry G. (1980). *What Will You Have to Drink?* Beaverlodge, Alberta, Canada: Horizon House.

Favazza, Armando R. (February 1983). Alcoholism. *American Family Physician,* pp. 274–78.

Feher, D. (1976). Psychotherapy. In M. R. Tarter and A. Superman (Eds.), *Alcoholism: Interdisciplinary Approaches to an Enduring Problem.* Reading, Mass.: Addison-Wesley, 1976.

Finer, J. J. (1972). Overmanagement of the Alcoholic Patient. *Journal of the American Medical Association* 219: 622.

Fleetwood, M. F., and Diethelm, O. (1951). Emotional and Bio-chemical Findings and Alcoholism. *American Journal of Psychiatry* 108: 433–38.

Forrest, G. G. (1975). *The Diagnosis and Treatment of Alcoholism.* Springfield, Ill.: Charles C. Thomas.

Giannini, James, A.; Price, William A.; and Giannini, Matthew C. (March 1986). Contemporary Drugs of Abuse. *American Family Physician,* vol. 33, no. 3.

Gitlow, Stanley E. (June 20, 1983). Alcoholism: The Primary Disease Concept. *Audio Digest Family Practice,* vol. 12, no. 12.

Gomez, Linda. (May 1984). America's 100 Years of Euphoria and Despair. *Life,* 57–68.

Hamburg, S. (1975). Behavior Therapy in Alcoholism: A Critical Review of Broad-Spectrum Approaches. *Journal of Studies on Alcohol* 36: 69–87.

Hayman, M. (1966). Alcoholism: *Mechanism and Management.* Springfield, Ill.: C. C. Thomas.

Hershorn, H. I. (1973). Alcoholism, Physical Dependence and Disease: Comment on "The Alcohologist's Addiction." *Quarterly Journal of Studies on Alcohol* 34: 506–8.

Jackson, D. (1957). The Question of Family Homeostasis. *Psychiatry Quarterly Supplement* 31: 79.

Jellinek, E. M. (1960). *The Disease Concept of Alcoholism.* Highland Park. N.J.: Hillhouse Press, 23.

The Kinds of Drugs Kids Are Getting Into. (1984). Pharmacists Against Drug Abuse (pamphlet). PADA 3841.

Krupp, Marcus A., and Chatton, Milton J., ed. (1981). *Current Medical Diagnosis and Treatment.* Los Altos: Lange Medical Publications, 645–48.

Meier, Paul D. (1982). *Introduction to Psychology & Counseling.* Grand Rapids, Mich.: Baker Book House.

Meyer, Roger E., (1980). Drug and Alcohol Addiction, Including Committing and Social Perspectives. *Survey of Psychiatry,* 31–33.

Miller, P. M.; Hersen, M.; Eisler, R. M.; Epstein, L. H.; and Wooten, L. S. (1974). Relationship of Alcohol Cues to the Drinking Behavior of Alcoholics and Social Drinkers: An Analogue Study. *The Psychological Record* 24: 61–66.

Miller, W. R., and Caddy, G. R. (1979). Abstinence and Controlled Drinking in the Treatment of Problem Drinkers. *Journal of Studies on Alcohol* 38(1): 980–1003.

Minuchin, S. (1979). Constructing a Therapeutic Reality. In E. Kaufman and P. N. Kaufman (eds.). *Family Therapy of Drug and Alcohol Abuse.* New York: Gardner Press.

Mirin, Steven M. (1977). Drug Addiction and Alcoholism. *Survey of Psychiatry,* 12–16.

National Commission on Marijuana and Drug Abuse. (March 1973). *Drug Use in America: Problem in Perspective* (Second Report). Washington D.C.: U.S. Government Printing Office.

National Institute on Alcohol Abuse and Alcoholism. (1975). *Occupational Alcoholism: Some Problems and Some Solutions.* Rockville, Md: National Institute on Alcohol Abuse and Alcoholism, U.S. Dept. of Health, Education, and Welfare.

Nicholi, A. M., Jr. Marijuana—Nontherapeutic Use of Psychoactive Drugs, card #270.

Pattison, E. M. (1979). The Selection and Treatment Modalities for the Alcoholic Patient. In J. H. Mendelson and N. K. Mello, eds., *The Diagnosis and Treatment of Alcoholism.* New York: McGraw-Hill.

Pokorny, A. D.; Miller, B. A.; Kanas, T.; and Valles, J. (1973). Effectiveness of Extended Aftercare in the Treatment of Alcoholism. *Quarterly Journal of Studies on Alcoholism* 34: 435–43.

Reilly, D. M. (1979). Drug Abusing Families: Intra Familial Dynamics and Brief Triphasic Treatment. In E. Kaufman and P. N. Kaufman (eds.). *Family Therapy of Drug and Alcohol Abuse.* New York: Gardner Press.

Reinert, R. E. (1968). The Concept of Alcoholism As a Disease. *Bulletin of the Menninger Clinic* 32: 21–25.

Reinert, R. E., and Bowmen, W. T. (1968). Social Drinking Following Treatment for Alcoholism. *Bulletin of the Menninger Clinic,* 32: 289–90.

Rotter, J. B. (1966). Generalized Expectancies for Internal Versus External Control of Reinforcements. *Psychological Monograph, General and Applied* 80: 1–28.

Rowe, Clarence J. (1980). *An Outline of Psychiatry.* Dubuque, Iowa: Wm. C. Brown Co., 161–71.

Senay, Edward C. (1985). Diagnosis and Management of Substance Abuse I. *Directions in Psychiatry* 5(33): 1–7.

Senay, Edward C. (1985). Diagnosis and Management of Substance Abuse III. *Directions in Psychiatry* 5(35): 1–6.

"Smoking Called Top Health Risk in Nation." (May 24, 1984). *Dallas Times Herald.*

Solomon, Philip and Patch, Vernon D. (1974). *Handbook of Psychiatry.* Los Altos: Lange Medical Publications, 314–29.

Spickard, Anderson and Thompson, Barbara R. (1985). *Dying for a Drink.* Waco, Tex.: Word Books, 69.

Stedman, T. L. (1962). *Stedman's Medical Dictionary* (20th ed.). Baltimore: The Williams and Wilkins Co., 27.

Steele, C. M.; Southwick, L. L.; and Critchlow, B. (1981). Dissonance and Alcohol: Drinking Your Troubles Away. *Journal of Personality and Social Psychology* 41(5): 831–46.

Steiner, C. (1971). *Games Alcoholics Play.* New York: Grove Press.

Tomb, David A. (1981). *Psychiatry for the House Officer.* Baltimore/London: Williams & Williams 122–26.

Viamontes, J. A. (1972). Review of Drug Effectiveness in the Treatment of Alcoholism. *American Journal of Psychiatry* 128: 1570–71.

Vista Hill Foundation. (April 1987). *Drug Abuse and Alcoholism Newsletter,* vol. 16, no. 4.

Westfield, D. R. (1972). Two Years' Experience of Group Methods in the Treatment of Male Alcoholics in a Scottish Mental Hospital. *British Journal of Addictions* 67: 267–76.

Wharton, Lawrence H. (June 6, 1983). The Great Stoned Age. *Audio-Digest Family Practice,* vol. 31, no.22.

Wolff, K. (1968). Hospitalized Alcoholic Patients III: Motivating Alcoholics Through Group Psychotherapy. *Hospital and Community Psychiatry* 19: 206–9.

Yancey, Philip (February 4, 1983). *Christianity Today.*

Ziegler-Driscoll, G. (1979). The Similarities in Families of Drug Dependents and Alcoholics. In E. Kaufman and P. N. Kaufman (eds.) *Family Therapy of Drug and Alcohol Abuse.* New York: Gardner Press.